THE
SECRET
OF THE
YELLOW
DEATH

THE SECRET OF THE YELLOW DEATH

A True Story of Medical Sleuthing

By Suzanne Jurmain

Houghton Mifflin Books for Children
Houghton Mifflin Harcourt
Boston   New York   2009

Houghton Mifflin Books for Children is an imprint of
Houghton Mifflin Harcourt Publishing Company.

www.hmhbooks.com

The book design is by YAY! Design.
The text of this book is set in Century Old Style.

Photo credits appear on page 98.

Library of Congress Cataloging-in-Publication Data

Jurmain, Suzanne.
The secret of the yellow death : a true story of medical sleuthing / by Suzanne Jurmain.
p. cm.
ISBN 978-0-618-96581-6
1. Yellow fever—Diagnosis—Cuba–Juvenile literature. 2. Yellow fever—Juvenile literature. I. Title.
RC212.C9J87 2009
614.5'41097291—dc22
2009022499

Printed in Singapore

TWP 10 9 8 7 6 5 4 3 2 1

To Dr. Jay Marks, Dr. Charles Burstin, and
Dr. Philip Brooks, with honor, gratitude, and deep appreciation.

ACKNOWLEDGMENTS

Two of the most important words in all the English language are "thank you," and I certainly owe thanks to the many people who made it possible for me to write this book.

As always, I am grateful to my agent, Edward Necarsulmer, for his encouragement and to my editor, Ann Rider, for her good ideas, cheering words, and thought-provoking comments.

Dr. Martha Sonnenberg kindly took time out of her busy schedule to answer my strange questions, and I must also extend my thanks to the librarians at the New York Academy of Medicine and the UCLA Biomedical Library who graciously allowed me to examine the material in their collections.

To Claudia Sueyras, a wonderful researcher at the University of Virginia, I owe a huge debt. She combed the archives, answered questions, sent me photographs, and was always ready to provide more help.

My heartfelt thanks must also go to Paul Song of Superior Galleries for providing photographs and information about the Congressional Gold Medal; to Professor Barbara Becker at the University of California, Irvine, who suggested sources for many of the photos; and to my son, David Jurmain, who came to my rescue with much-needed computer expertise.

Robert Scott moved heaven and earth to find me examples of the postage stamps showing Dr. Finlay; and my brother, David Tripp, provided contacts, source material, and, as always, a shoulder to lean on.

Finally, my greatest thanks must go to my husband, Richard, who took photos, answered questions, provided comfort, and reminded me time and time again through his own personal actions that doctors really can be heroes.

Walter Reed
(1851–1902)

Jesse Lazear
(1869–1900)

FIVE
DOCTORS
WHO SEARCHED
FOR THE
YELLOW FEVER
SECRET

James Carroll
(1854–1907)

Aristides Agramonte
(1869–1931)

Carlos Finlay
(1833–1915)

CONTENTS

A Note to the Reader

Just over one hundred years ago a band of
scientists and volunteers from two countries
decided to fight against one of the world's
deadliest diseases. Some members of this
group came from Cuba; some, from the
United States. Unfortunately, today relatively
little is known about the Cubans who took
part in this important battle, while libraries
contain many rich sources of information
about the American team. For this reason,
I have concentrated on the extremely well
documented American part of the story.
But readers should remember that without
the great Cuban scientific contribution,
there might have been no story to tell.

CHAPTER 1

MEETING THE MONSTER

Summer 1899

The young man didn't feel well. First, there was the chill: an icy, bone-freezing chill in the middle of a warm summer evening. Then there was the terrible crushing headache. His back hurt. His stomach twisted with pain. And then he was hot, boiling hot, with a fever that hovered around 104 degrees. His skin turned yellow. The whites of his eyes looked like lemons. Nauseated, he gagged and threw up again and again, spewing streams of vomit black with digested clots of blood across the pillow. Sometimes he cried out or babbled in delirium. Violent spasms jolted his body. It took two grown men to hold him in his bed as a nurse wiped away the drops of blood that trickled from his nose and mouth. Nights and mornings passed. Then, five days after that first freezing chill, the young man died: another victim of a terrible disease called yellow fever.

○○○○○

1

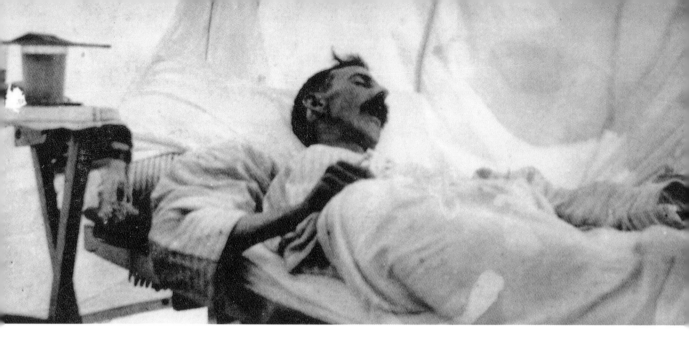

A yellow fever patient in a Cuban hospital around 1900.

Doctors didn't know what caused it. They couldn't cure it. But they knew that yellow fever was a killer. For centuries the disease had swept through parts of the Americas and Africa, leaving behind a trail of loss and misery. It turned cities into ghost towns and left the local graveyards filled with corpses. In New Orleans, Dr. Kennedy took sick and collapsed while he was tending patients. In Philadelphia, Dr. Hodge's little girl caught the fever, turned yellow, and died in two short days. And when the sickness killed the Memphis snack shop woman Kate Bionda, she left behind her husband and two small children. The fever struck the rich. It struck the poor. It killed the humble, and it humbled the important. Jefferson Davis, president of the Confederate States of America during the U.S. Civil War, lost his son to yellow fever. George Clymer, who'd signed the Declaration of Independence, watched helplessly as the sickness struck his wife and family. And every single year the illness took its toll. In 1793, 4,044 people in Philadelphia died during a plague of yellow fever. New Orleans counted 8,101 yellow fever deaths in 1853. And when the disease hit Memphis, Tennessee, in 1878, 17,000 citizens sickened in a single month. Stores closed. Work stopped. Thousands fled, and those who remained wandered through a nightmare city—where sick children huddled next to dying parents and hungry dogs roamed the silent streets searching for their lost dead masters.

"Yellow fever [is] . . . an enemy which imperils life and cripples commerce and industry," Surgeon General John Woodworth told the U.S. Congress in 1879. And he was right. In one single century—between 1800 and 1900—the disease sickened approximately 500,000 U.S. citizens and killed about 100,000.

The question was, what could be done about it?

By the 1890s doctors had found that many illnesses are caused by one-celled microscopic organisms called bacteria. With the help of this new knowledge, they taught the public how to kill these dangerous bacterial "germs" with things like heat and disinfectant. They also learned how to use dead or weakened germs to make vaccines—special types of medicine that prevent illness by forcing a living body to produce its own disease-fighting substances. Slowly, physicians began to conquer deadly sicknesses like cholera, typhoid, anthrax, and diphtheria. But yellow fever still raged. Researchers studied the disease. Doctors argued about the cause. Scientists peered through their microscopes, looking for the yellow fever germ. But there was no progress. Each year the hot summer weather brought on yellow fever epidemics. Each year desperate people burned clothing, bedding, and even buildings that had housed yellow fever victims in hopes of stopping the disease. Frantic doctors bled the sick, stuck them in mustard baths, dosed them with opium, or gave them drugs that might make them vomit out the germ—but nothing helped. Each year thousands of people caught the disease. Thousands died of it. And then, suddenly, something happened—something that at first didn't seem to have anything to do with yellow fever or with medical science.

On February 9, 1898, the U.S. battleship *Maine* blew up in the harbor of Havana, Cuba. Two hundred and sixty-eight American servicemen were killed. U.S. officials told a shocked nation that Spanish government agents had deliberately caused the explosion. And by the end of April the United States had decided to go to war with Spain.

3

U.S. soldiers prepare to board a ship that will take them to Cuba to fight in the Spanish-American War.

In the next four months American soldiers beat the Spanish army in Cuba. They beat the Spanish navy in the Pacific. And when the Spanish-American War ended in July, the victorious U.S. forces had won the right to govern Cuba and Puerto Rico (two islands off the southern coast of Florida), as well as the Pacific Ocean islands of Guam and the Philippines. Unfortunately, the war had also brought the United States face-to-face with another deadly enemy: yellow fever.

Because of the disease, the newly conquered Cuban territory was a deathtrap. Yellow fever epidemics swept the country. Visitors often contracted the illness soon after landing on the island's shores. Some U.S. troops had already died of the disease in Cuba, and Washington officials were alarmed.

In 1900 yellow fever (sometimes called yellow jack)
was viewed as a monster. In this cartoon
the monster is killing a woman who represents the state
of Florida while another woman (labeled "Columbia")
who represents the United States cries for help.

What would happen to American soldiers in Cuba if a full-scale epidemic broke out on the island? Or, worse, what would happen if homecoming U.S. troops carried yellow fever back to North America? That was the kind of thinking that gave United States officials nightmares.

Something had to be done.

Somehow the country had to find a way to prevent more attacks of yellow fever.

But before U.S. scientists could stop or cure the disease, they had to understand it. They had to know what caused the sickness. They had to know what spread it. And it was important that they find out soon.

On May 24, 1900, the U.S. government sent orders to four American army doctors. Their mission was to go to Cuba and find the cause of yellow fever.

CHAPTER 2

"FEEDING THE FISHES"

June 21–24, 1900

The USS *Sedgwick* lurched, and Major Walter Reed, M.D., promptly threw up. The ship was barely out of New York. Already he was seasick. And now, now that he was facing the biggest, most important challenge of his whole career, Dr. Walter Reed didn't need to waste time leaning over the rail and doing what he called "feeding the fishes."

For roughly twenty years, Reed had dreamed of being able to do something big, something important, something that he hoped would "alleviate human suffering." It was a dream he'd had when he was a young army doctor tending settlers, soldiers, and Apaches on lonely frontier outposts. It was something he'd thought about when he went back to school at age thirty-nine to study bacteriology—a brand-new branch of medical science that dealt with the disease-causing germs that researchers called bacteria. For ten more years Reed had hoped to make a major contribution while he did research and taught students at the U.S. Army Medical School in Washington, D.C. And now, finally, at age forty-nine, he had a chance to take on the most exciting and important project of his whole career. Just a few weeks earlier, the U.S. Army had ordered Dr. Walter Reed to go to Cuba, head a team of three other doctors, and find the cause of yellow fever. But where was he going to start?

Before leaving Washington, Reed had read the latest medical books and done some preliminary experiments. He'd looked at scientific articles on yellow fever, and he'd also talked to people who'd spent time studying the illness. By now he knew that there were several current theories on the cause of the disease, and he could tick off on his fingers the first three items that had to be investigated.

First was an idea suggested by Dr. Giuseppe Sanarelli. A few years earlier this Italian researcher had

Photograph of Walter Reed at age thirty-one, about twenty years before he began his work on yellow fever.

announced that a type of bacteria called *Bacillus icteroides* was the cause of yellow fever. That sounded good. But Reed's recent experiments had shown that *Bacillus icteroides* actually caused a pig disease called hog cholera. Now scientists were arguing about which research results were right, and Walter Reed knew that his team would have to find a way of settling the issue. That was a big project, and it was only the beginning.

Next on the list was an old theory—one that had been around for years. It claimed that healthy people got the disease by touching clothing, bedding, or furniture that had been used by yellow fever patients. That idea was so popular that it had appeared in medical books. Many health authorities believed it. So did many doctors. Of course, no scientist had ever proved the theory to be true. But it was definitely a matter for Reed and his assistants to consider.

8

And then, finally, there was another idea. A very different one. For almost twenty years, in more than one hundred experiments, a Cuban doctor named Carlos Finlay had tried to prove that mosquito bites caused yellow fever. Time and time again, the Cuban scientist had attempted to show that bugs could carry the disease by letting mosquitoes he thought might be infected with the germ bite groups of healthy patients. But none of Finlay's patients ever developed a truly clear-cut case of yellow fever from the bites. The experiments were unsuccessful. Many scientists laughed at the Cuban doctor's failures. The mosquito theory didn't seem to fit the facts, and no one understood why Finlay still continued to believe it. Maybe, some people said, the Cuban doctor was "touched." Others came right out and called him "crazy." Even Reed's boss, the surgeon general of the army, George Sternberg—a leading American bacteriologist—thought that the mosquito theory was a joke. Investigating it was "useless," he told Reed. And there was a good chance that the army surgeon general was right. Most sensible scientists did

Carlos Finlay, the Cuban doctor who tried to prove that mosquito bites caused yellow fever.

think the mosquito theory sounded pretty flaky. And *Bacillus icteroides*? Well, because of his own research, Reed privately thought that was probably pretty flaky, too.

But, of course, what Reed *thought* didn't matter. Science wasn't about opinions or theories. It was about facts. And Reed's job was clear. With the help of his team, he had to find the facts. He had to test each one of the theories. He had to find out—once and for all—if any of them was right. And if all three current theories were wrong, Reed would have to come up with a new idea— and test that. It was a big job. A tough one. But if Reed and his team could do it . . . if somehow they could find the cause of yellow fever, it might help scientists prevent the disease—or cure it.

But that was all in the future.

At the moment, the only cure Reed really needed was a remedy for seasickness. In a letter to his wife and daughter, he said that there seemed to be "two or three tons of brick in . . . [his] stomach."

And when the USS *Sedgwick* rolled again, Dr. Walter Reed leaned over, threw up, and "fed the fishes."

CHAPTER 3

PLANS

June 25, 1900

The sun was warm. The sea was blue. The orange juice, black coffee, and dry toast had stayed down. And Walter Reed was standing at the rail watching as his ship steamed past wharves, past the wreck of the battleship *Maine,* and into the harbor of Havana, Cuba.

When the ship docked at around eleven, Reed was ready to move. An epidemic of yellow fever had recently broken out in the Cuban town of Quemados. Some people in Havana were also sick with the disease. Even the chief U.S. medical officer for Western Cuba, Reed's good friend Major Jefferson Kean, had come down with the illness several days earlier. There was no time to waste.

*The hospital tents, nurses, and other medical personnel at Camp Columbia
as they looked about a year before Reed arrived.*

Reed quickly loaded his bags into a carriage and drove through the
bustling city streets of Havana and across eight miles of country roads until he
reached the U.S. Army post at Camp Columbia. After dropping his bags at the
Officers' Quarters, he was off again, dashing across the grounds to visit Major
Kean in the camp's yellow fever hospital just outside the base.

There the news was good. Kean's case was fairly mild. He was expected
to live. At the bedside Reed probably chatted like any other visitor, but he
must have also assessed the patient with a scientific eye. Was Kean's skin
yellow? Was his temperature high? Were his gums bleeding? What had he been
doing in the days before he got sick? Had he been near mosquitoes? Infected
clothing? Reed had read descriptions of yellow fever, but this was the first live
case he'd ever seen. He was hungry for information. He wanted clues. But he

FIELD HOSPITAL 1ST DIVISION 7TH ARMY CORPS. CAPACITY 500 BEDS. CAMP COLUMBIA — HAVANA CUBA. MAR. 1899. VIEW FROM CENTER OF HOSPITAL SHOWING 3 COMPANIES OF THE HOSPITAL CORPS DETACHMENT AND WOMEN NURSES.

couldn't spend the rest of the day at Kean's bedside. If Reed was going to get the research started, he had to organize his team.

The first meeting had already been called, and late in the afternoon Reed walked onto the garden patio outside Camp Columbia's Officers' Quarters to greet the three men he'd be working with.

They were all there, formally dressed in their crisp white tropical army uniforms. On one side was the tall, thin, balding Dr. James Carroll, a blunt, outwardly charmless man who seemed to be more comfortable looking through a microscope than making conversation. Near Carroll was the chatty Cuban-born, U.S.-educated Dr. Aristides Agramonte, looking like a dandy with his pointed, curled mustache. And rounding out the group was the quiet, bearded, darkly handsome Dr. Jesse W. Lazear.

All of the men had graduated from medical school. All had studied bacteriology, and together they brought a wealth of talent to the project. Carroll 13

The wreck of the U.S. battleship Maine *as it probably looked when Reed sailed into the harbor at Havana, Cuba. Reed told his wife that it made his blood "boil" when he remembered the explosion that destroyed "those brave men & gallant ship."*

had a real passion for lab work. Agramonte, an honors graduate of Columbia University Medical School, had already spent time investigating yellow fever. And Lazear, a former college football player who'd studied medicine in both the United States and Europe, had headed one of the clinical labs at America's prestigious Johns Hopkins University. All three men had worked with Reed in the past, and they listened intently as the chief scientist outlined his program.

The first job, Reed told his colleagues, was to prove that *Bacillus icteroides* was—or was not—the cause of yellow fever.

That would take a lot of lab work, and each scientist would have his own specific job.

14   Agramonte would do autopsies. He'd surgically open the bodies of dead

yellow fever victims and take out samples of blood, stomach, heart, kidney, and other organ tissues.

Carroll, the best bacteriologist, would take those samples to the lab. He would place tiny amounts of the tissue Agramonte harvested in tubes or dishes filled with a food substance like gelatin or bouillon. Then he would watch to see if any of the tissue samples grew *Bacillus icteroides* or any other bacteria that might prove to be the cause of yellow fever.

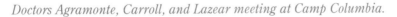

Lazear would help examine the bacteria and tissues under a microscope.

Reed would coordinate the work and help out wherever he could. That covered the important points. But there was one thing more. As he looked around at his assistants, Reed said that he hoped the group would stick closely to his plan. Finding the cause of yellow fever was a tremendous challenge, and he wanted the men to combine their efforts and attack the problem as a team.

Doctors Agramonte, Carroll, and Lazear meeting at Camp Columbia.

Everyone agreed. Work was scheduled to start the following morning. And, as they left the meeting, the four men must have known they were about to start a very dangerous project. People who had had yellow fever were immune. They couldn't possibly get the disease again. But none of the men on Reed's team had ever had a full-blown attack of yellow fever. Reed had certainly never had the disease. Neither had Lazear or Carroll. Though there was a chance that the Cuban-born Agramonte might have had a very mild case as a small child, he was not definitely immune. And all four doctors knew that by being on the fever-stricken island of Cuba, by coming close to sick patients, and by studying bacteria in the lab, they were running a serious risk of getting yellow fever.

Dr. Jesse Lazear (standing seventh from the right wearing a cap and mustache) with his college football team in the 1890s. Lazear, who studied medicine in Europe and the United States, was both a scholar and an athlete.

CHAPTER 4

GOING NOWHERE

Early July 1900

The lab didn't look like much. It was an old wooden shack at Camp Columbia, stuffed with wooden tables, shelves, jars, flasks, test tubes, a hot oven for sterilizing, an incubator to provide the warmth needed for growing bacteria, and a couple of microscopes. From morning until lunch, from lunch until dinner, Reed and Carroll worked side by side, juggling tubes and peering through microscope lenses. Lazear came and went, taking his turn at studying the steady stream of tissue specimens Agramonte sent from his autopsy lab in Havana.

The problem seemed simple. If *Bacillus icteroides* caused yellow fever, it ought to be found in the bodies of yellow fever victims. All Reed and his colleagues had to do was look. So, as the warm July days sped past, the four doctors searched for *Bacillus icteroides* in blood samples that had been taken from live yellow fever patients. They also tried to find the bacteria in blood and bits of tissue that had been taken from the dead. With delicate loops made of platinum wire they streaked infected blood onto gelatin-filled plates and popped these cultures in the incubator to see if warmth and the gelatin food would make Dr. Giuseppe Sanarelli's mysterious bacteria grow. They tried to grow the bacteria by placing tiny samples of the livers, spleens, kidneys,

17

intestines, and hearts of yellow fever victims in test tubes filled with bouillon that bacteria liked to eat. But nothing much grew in the tubes or on the plates. And no matter how carefully the men looked through their microscopes, they couldn't find a single sample of *Bacillus icteroides*.

Yet yellow fever was all around the team that summer. Men and women in Havana were dying of the disease. American officers were coming down with yellow fever, even though Walter Reed never mentioned that in personal letters.

Almost every day, he sat down at the long wooden table in his quarters and wrote a cheerful, chatty letter to his "precious wife," Emilie. He told her

At the beginning of the twentieth century, laboratories had simple equipment and no air conditioning. The Reed team's lab at Camp Columbia probably looked a lot like this 1917 hospital laboratory.

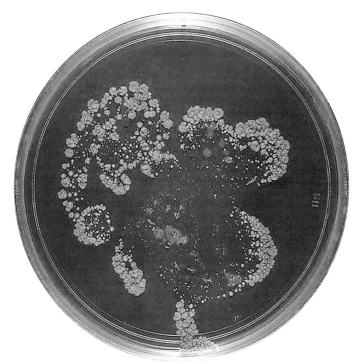

A modern photo showing
millions of bacteria growing
in clusters on a glass plate
filled with gelatin.
The Reed team hoped to find
the yellow fever germ
by growing bacteria on plates
like this.

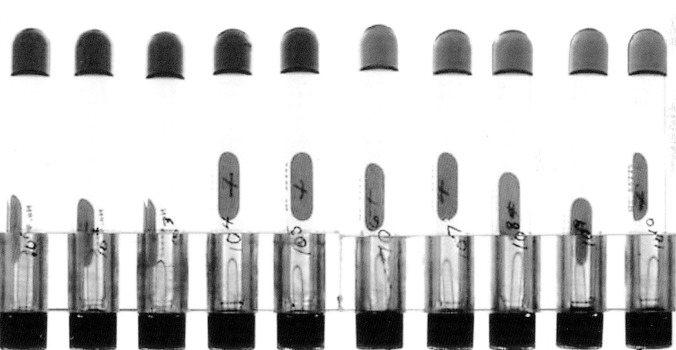

A modern photo showing test tubes filled with bouillon.
Bouillon is an excellent food for bacteria, and the Reed team hoped it would
help them grow samples of the mysterious yellow fever germ.

19

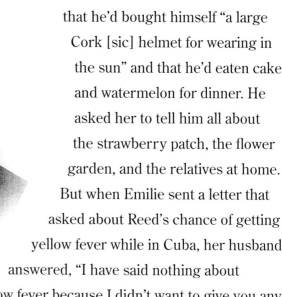

that he'd bought himself "a large Cork [sic] helmet for wearing in the sun" and that he'd eaten cake and watermelon for dinner. He asked her to tell him all about the strawberry patch, the flower garden, and the relatives at home. But when Emilie sent a letter that asked about Reed's chance of getting yellow fever while in Cuba, her husband answered, "I have said nothing about yellow fever because I didn't want to give you any worry, especially as I wasn't taking any risks whatever."

No risks whatever?

The truth was, all of Reed's activities were risky.

But, apparently, Reed didn't want his wife to know it. When he wrote his letters home, Reed didn't tell Emilie that yellow fever was sweeping across Cuba. He didn't say that he might get the illness from handling infected tissue specimens. And he also didn't mention one other troubling fact: the team was making very little progress.

By the middle of July, Reed and his colleagues had produced dozens of gelatin cultures and bouillon preparations. They had spent hours looking at organ tissue under the microscope. But they couldn't find *Bacillus icteroides*—or any other type of germ that might possibly be the cause of yellow fever.

That bothered Dr. Jesse Lazear.

At work the former football player always did his job. To team members, he was always "pleasant" and "polite." In his spare time, he wrote cheery letters home, telling his pregnant wife about the tropical rain and the funny way that the charmless Dr. Carroll's ears stuck out. But sometimes, when he sat alone, writing to his family, Lazear couldn't hold his feelings back. The laboratory work wasn't going well, he reported. The project was getting nowhere. And as for his teammates . . . Well, it wasn't Carroll's ears he was concerned about. It was Carroll. The tall, balding bacteriologist had a "dull" expression. He didn't seem imaginative. All he seemed to care about was studying "germs for their own sake." And Reed? Reed seemed to be stuck. All he seemed to care about, Lazear wrote, was hunting for *Bacillus icteroides*. But Lazear thought that looking for the strange bacillus was a waste of time. A dead end. To make progress, the team needed a new direction. And Jesse Lazear had ideas—good ideas—about what that direction ought to be. Unfortunately, the rest of the team didn't seem to be taking those ideas very seriously. "I . . . want to do work which may lead to the discovery of the real organism," Lazear told his wife.

Dr. James Carroll. Carroll worked as Reed's assistant in Washington, D.C., before coming to Cuba.

But how could he? Reed gave the orders. Lazear had to obey. Nothing seemed likely to change.

And then, quite suddenly, something happened.

CHAPTER 5

THE FIRST CLUE?

Mid–Late July 1900

On one hot summer day, the team got word that American soldiers were dying of an illness at the Pinar del Rio army post, located about one hundred miles from Camp Columbia in Cuba. But was the sickness yellow fever? No one seemed to know, and army officials ordered Dr. Agramonte to investigate.

It was a good choice. Agramonte, a charming and sophisticated man, was also a very smart, well-qualified physician. He'd examined plenty of living yellow fever patients. He'd autopsied the bodies of those who'd died of the disease. He knew all the symptoms of the illness, and he headed to Pinar del Rio right away.

One of the sick soldiers had died just hours before Agramonte reached the camp. The body was waiting, and Agramonte promptly did an autopsy.

As he worked, the doctor looked for the usual signs of yellow fever: the yellow eyes, the yellowish liver, the yellow skin, all of which were caused by serious damage to the liver. Since liver injury can prevent the blood from clotting and because yellow fever can also make the body's veins and arteries "leak," Agramonte thoroughly checked the corpse for signs of bleeding. Was there liquid blood in parts of the digestive tract? Partially digested blood that looked like coffee grounds inside the stomach? One by one, the doctor noted down his findings, and by the time he put his scalpel down, Agramonte knew one thing for certain. The soldier on the table had died of yellow fever.

After leaving the autopsy room, the doctor walked through the camp's hospital ward, moving carefully from bed to bed. To his horror, there were more patients showing telltale signs of yellow fever. There was no mistaking

Dr. Aristides Agramonte, the only member of the Reed team born in Cuba, was the son of a Cuban general who died fighting against the Spanish for Cuban independence.

the yellow skin and eyes, the bleeding gums, the high temperatures, and the slow pulse rates. Somehow the doctors at Pinar del Rio had failed to recognize a yellow fever outbreak.

Agramonte immediately telegraphed the news to headquarters. Reed jumped on a train the following morning. By July 21 he had joined his colleague at the camp, and the two men began to search for the cause of the disease.

The statistics were clear. Thirty-five soldiers at the army post had come down with yellow fever. Eleven had been killed by the vicious illness. How had all those young Americans become infected?

One man, a prisoner who'd been locked up in the guardhouse, had died of the disease. But he hadn't been near any yellow fever patients before or during his imprisonment. He hadn't ever touched clothes or sheets that had been used by other yellow fever victims. How could he possibly have gotten sick? And what about the eight other men who shared his cell? They had breathed the same air the sick man had breathed. They had touched his clothes, brushed against his blankets, and handled his dishes. But those eight men had stayed completely well.

So what had caused the dead prisoner's attack of yellow fever?

Reed and Agramonte examined the possibilities.

It wasn't *Bacillus icteroides*. That much was clear. After weeks of work, the team had found no evidence that Sanarelli's bacteria had anything to do with yellow fever. That eliminated one theory.

Contact with infected clothing and bedding didn't seem to have spread the disease to the dead prisoner's cellmates. That discredited the idea that yellow fever was somehow spread by touch.

So where had the disease come from? And how had it managed to strike only one soldier in a locked guardhouse?

That was a mystery, but wrapped inside that mystery was a clue.

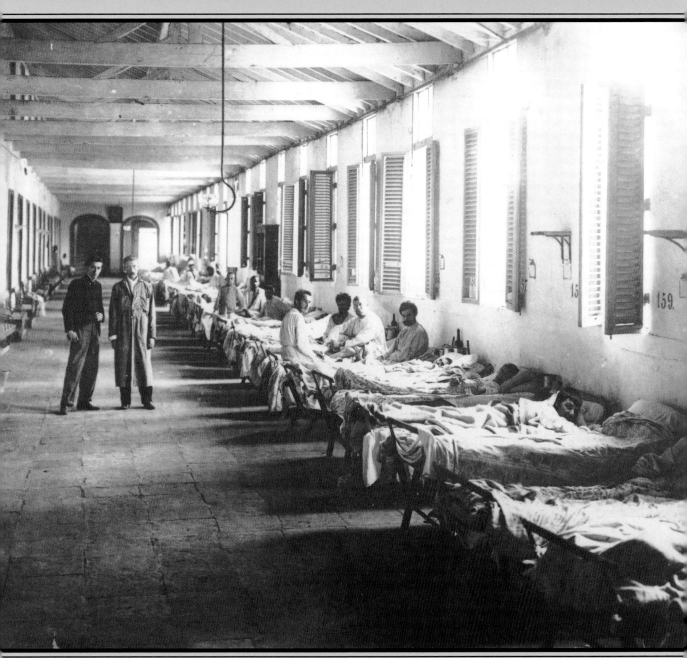

Patients in a Havana yellow fever hospital in 1899. The ward Dr. Agramonte walked through at Pinar del Rio probably looked a lot like this.

CHAPTER 6

BUGS

Late July 1900

After weeks of work, the team had finally found a clue, and it was just the kind of clue Jesse Lazear probably had hoped for. It fit in with his private thoughts exactly, because for the last few months—while Reed, Carroll, and Agramonte had been focused on finding *Bacillus icteroides*—Dr. Jesse Lazear had been thinking about bugs.

Since May 1900 he'd been studying insects and considering the possible relationship between yellow fever and mosquitoes. Scientific articles had taught him that biting ticks could spread the deadly Texas fever germ through an entire herd of cattle. From reading, Lazear had also learned that mosquitoes infected with a tiny microbe could transmit the sickness that people called malaria. If insects could spread the tiny germs that caused those two diseases, he reasoned, there was a good chance they could carry the germ of yellow fever, too. Right from the start, Lazear had wanted the team to do mosquito research. But none of the other doctors had seemed particularly interested.

Until now.

Now all four doctors were willing to admit that something must have carried yellow fever through the bars of that Pinar del Rio guardhouse. Something had allowed the disease to strike a single prisoner. And that something *could* have been a mosquito.

It was time to investigate further, and the first step was to consult an expert.

At some time, possibly in late July, members of the Reed team drove up to a house on Aguacate Street in Havana. They had come to visit Dr. Carlos Finlay, the Cuban scientist who had tried for years to prove that mosquitoes carried yellow fever. For decades medical researchers around the world had laughed at "crazy" Dr. Finlay and his lunatic ideas. But the formally dressed, white-whiskered gentleman who greeted the Americans didn't seem like a mad scientist. He was a dignified, highly educated, bespectacled sixty-seven-year-old who knew six languages—including English—and spoke all of them with a slight stutter. During the day, Dr. Finlay treated patients—whether or not they could afford to pay. At night, he devoted time to scientific research. For twenty

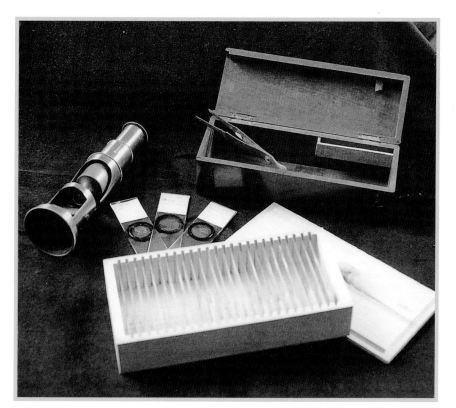

Dr. Jesse Lazear's pocket microscope and slides. Lazear was studying the relationship between mosquitoes and yellow fever before Reed reached Cuba, and he may have used this microscope to examine insects as part of his research.

27

years he'd ignored the rude remarks that others made about his work on yellow fever. For twenty years he'd continued to believe his theory. And now he was eager to share his thoughts with the others.

Yellow fever, he told the team, was probably spread by the bite of one particular kind of mosquito—a striped insect that was called the *Aedes aegypti* (pronounced *a-dees egypti*) mosquito by scientists.

That was the first point.

The second point, Dr. Finlay noted, was that mosquitoes—including *Aedes aegypti*—spread disease by sucking blood.

When a mosquito bites, it is actually using its long, needlelike nose (called a proboscis) to stab through the skin and draw blood from its victim. If the mosquito bites a sick person, it sucks in germ-infected blood. Later, when that infected mosquito bites again, it uses its proboscis to inject those germs into a healthy person's body.

The process is simple, but only a female mosquito can carry it out— because only a female mosquito is capable of sucking blood.

As a rule, both males and females eat plant juice and fruit nectar. Females, however, also need blood meals to help them manufacture the thousands of eggs that they lay in ponds, pools, puddles, and containers of still water.

To illustrate this point, Dr. Finlay handed the Americans a batch of tiny black "cigar-shaped" specks. They were dried *Aedes aegypti* eggs that he had recently

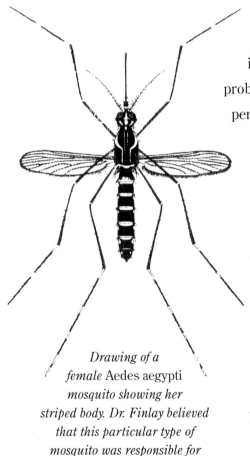

Drawing of a female Aedes aegypti *mosquito showing her striped body. Dr. Finlay believed that this particular type of mosquito was responsible for spreading yellow fever.*

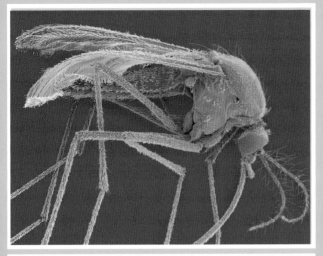

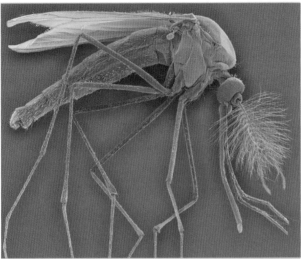

Highly magnified photos showing male and female mosquitoes of a type called Culex pipiens. *The female (top), like all female mosquitoes, has a long nose (called a proboscis) that allows her to stab through skin and draw blood. The male (bottom), like all male mosquitoes, has bushy antennae on his head that make him look different from the female. Although most mosquitoes are brown, black, gray, or tan, these photos have been artificially colored so that the body parts of the mosquito can be seen more clearly.*

scooped out of a bowl of water in his own library. If those eggs were placed in water and kept relatively warm, Finlay told the team, they would grow into adult mosquitoes in about two weeks.

The visit had been enormously helpful. As they left Finlay's Havana house, carrying the batch of mosquito eggs, the Americans must have been excited. There was a new theory to test. There were new experiments to plan. But, excited or not, the team still wasn't ready to devote all its energy to bugs. Carroll, who still had serious doubts about the mosquito theory, would keep on working with his microscope in hopes of finding the actual yellow fever germ. Agramonte would continue to do autopsies of yellow fever victims because their bodies might hold some new, important clue. Reed wouldn't be able to do much initially because he had to spend a few weeks in the United States, finishing up a report on typhoid fever that he had started earlier. That left Lazear—whose passionate interest made him the perfect person to take charge of the new mosquito research program.

First, he would hatch the eggs that Dr. Finlay had provided and raise a crop of *Aedes aegypti* mosquitoes that had never been exposed to any illness. Then he would have the females bite a group of yellow fever patients so that the disease-free bugs could pick up the infection. Finally, to prove that the insects could actually carry the disease germ, Dr. Lazear would have to allow female *Aedes aegypti* mosquitoes that had bitten yellow fever patients to bite healthy animals or humans. Then he would have to see if the healthy creatures developed the disease.

And that was a problem. As far as the team knew, animals didn't get yellow fever. That meant the infected mosquitoes would have to bite a group of people.

But who? Who was going to be bitten?

The decision would have to be made soon. Reed had to return to the United States August 2, and it was important to get the new mosquito research started.

On the night of August 1—when, for some unknown reason, Agramonte was not present—Reed, Carroll, and Lazear met at Camp Columbia. They discussed the problem and decided that all three of them would volunteer for the experiments.

Of course, if Carlos Finlay and Jesse Lazear were right—if mosquitoes did carry the disease germs—a human volunteer bitten by an infected bug could get yellow fever and die of the disease. That was the risk. But all three doctors were prepared to face it. To fight the illness they were ready to take what Dr. Carroll later called "a soldier's chances."

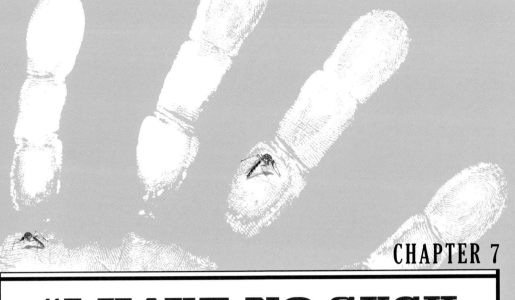

CHAPTER 7

"I HAVE NO SUCH THING"

August 1–30, 1900

It sounded so simple. All Lazear had to do was put the mosquito eggs in water, keep the water in a warm place, and wait a couple of weeks until the eggs hatched and grew into mature insects.

But it wasn't that easy. Some eggs just floated on the water and didn't hatch. Some insects died before they were completely grown up. Others dropped dead almost as soon as they became adults. Still, Lazear didn't give up. He tended his mosquitoes as if they were babies. Each day, he checked the progress of his little group. He made sure the adult insects were fed sweetened water and bits of banana. Sometimes he even let the females bite him and his lab attendants to make sure that they had nourishing drinks of blood. At last, when the insects were fully grown, Dr. Lazear put each mature female in a test tube. He plugged the opening with a fluffy cotton stopper and carried his tubes of mosquitoes to the yellow fever wards at Las Animas Hospital in Havana.

31

Two unknown people standing outside Las Animas Hospital in Havana, Cuba.
Since many yellow fever patients were taken to Las Animas,
members of the Reed team often did autopsies and experiments there.

On the hot August days, Lazear walked through the wards, stopping occasionally at a yellow fever patient's bedside to let one of his female mosquitoes bite.

It was a delicate process. First he turned the tube upside down so that the mosquito would fly upward into the glass end of the tube. Then Lazear swiftly removed the cotton plug and placed the open end of the tube flat on the patient's arm or belly. Patiently, he watched as the mosquito settled, inserted its proboscis through the skin, and sucked. After that, Lazear waited until the insect flew toward the top of the container. Then he picked up the tube, replaced the stopper, and noted down the date, the name of the patient who had been bitten, the number of days the patient had been ill, and the severity of the case. After several days passed, he let each one of these "infected" mosquitoes bite himself or another healthy volunteer.

But nothing happened. No one got sick.

Was the mosquito theory wrong? Was it another dead end?

The results were discouraging. Scientific progress, however, doesn't usually happen overnight, and Jesse Lazear was trying to be patient. Day after day, he tended his bugs. He wrote up his notes, and—even when he wasn't thinking about bugs—he must have worried. Far away, back in the States, his wife was lying in a hospital, suffering through complications of her second pregnancy. The baby was due any day, and Jesse Lazear was waiting for news.

August 15 passed. Then August 20. Finally, on August 25 a telegram arrived. Dr. Lazear's wife had successfully given birth to their second child, a baby girl. Of course, Lazear wouldn't actually get to meet his new daughter until he went home for a few weeks of leave in October. But it was a wonderful thing to think about. And by the end of August, Jesse Lazear probably needed all the wonderful thoughts that he could get, because his insect experiments were going very badly.

For weeks Lazear had pinned his hopes on the mosquito theory. For

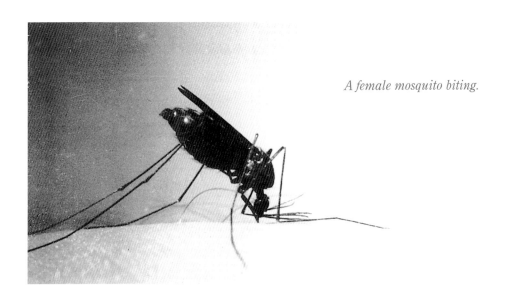

A female mosquito biting.

33

weeks he'd waited for a breakthrough. But by August 25 Jesse Lazear had tried to use mosquitoes to produce yellow fever in healthy people on nine distinct occasions. All his experiments had failed. Many of his bugs had died. Almost every day there were new frustrations, and the events on August 27 were all too typical. On that day an insect, one that had bitten a yellow fever patient on the second day of his sickness twelve days earlier, refused to bite another volunteer at Las Animas Hospital. Worse still, the bug looked weak. Lazear figured it would probably spoil his experiment by dying before morning, but he brought it back to the laboratory at Camp Columbia anyway.

Carroll was in the lab when Lazear came in, and the two men began to chat about the insect work. The truth was the mosquitoes seemed absolutely "harmless." Keeping them alive had become a major nuisance—and, in passing, Lazear told Carroll how his sickly bug had behaved that very morning.

Carroll had never believed in the mosquito theory, but he could easily see his colleague needed help. Since there was a chance that blood would help perk up the little insect, Carroll offered to let the feeble bug bite him.

At two p.m. Lazear turned the test tube upside down on Carroll's arm. He held it in place, and waited for the feeble mosquito to fly down and suck.

But the bug refused to settle. It fluttered here and there, landing again and again on the smooth sides of the tube. Minutes passed. The two men waited. Then, finally, Carroll took the tube out of Lazear's hand. He held it against his own arm and sat there patiently until, at last, the insect landed, bit, and drank its fill.

 That took care of that.

Lazear put his test tubes full of bugs away, and Carroll went on with his lab work.

Later that week, on August 30, James Carroll and Alva Pinto, another army doctor, went down to a nearby beach to take a swim. The water was warm, but suddenly Carroll felt a chill. Moments later he had a headache—a fierce

headache that seemed to be burning a hole straight through his brain. The pain was terrible, and by the time Carroll pulled himself out of the ocean, he didn't look well. Dr. Pinto glanced in his direction, saw the bacteriologist, and made an instant diagnosis. "Yellow fever," he said succinctly.

"Don't be a . . . fool," Carroll responded. "I have no such thing."

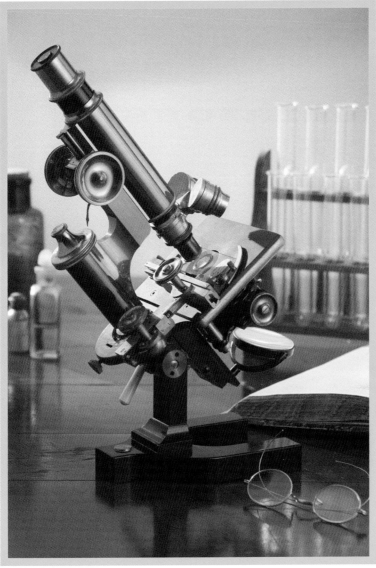

©*Tetra Images*

Modern photo of a hundred-year-old microscope. Dr. Carroll probably used a microscope like this for research.

CHAPTER 8

DELIRIOUS?

August 31–September 4, 1900

Of course, James Carroll had always known that Cuba was full of dangerous diseases. He'd known that coming to the island was a risk. And, yes, the bite from Lazear's sickly little bug could possibly have given him the fever. But James Carroll had never believed in the mosquito theory. He'd never thought that insects carried the disease. Besides, he couldn't afford to get the illness. He was a forty-six-year-old married man with five small children to support—and yellow fever often killed people over forty.

Still, there was no getting around the fact that his temperature was rising. Something was making him sick. And he needed to know exactly what the illness was.

It might be malaria. That could cause high fevers. It was a bad disease; but, still, it could be treated. It wasn't usually as deadly as yellow fever. Besides, malaria was often found in Cuba. Carroll could have picked up the infection. And the scientist knew there was an easy way of finding out.

Early in the morning on August 31, James Carroll dragged himself over to the lab. He jabbed himself with a needle and drew some blood. Then he smeared it on a glass slide and put the slide under the microscope. Carefully, he peered through the eyepiece, focused the lenses, and began to look.

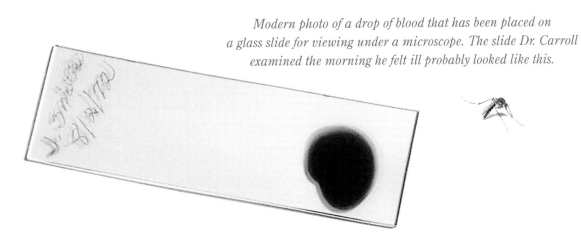

Modern photo of a drop of blood that has been placed on a glass slide for viewing under a microscope. The slide Dr. Carroll examined the morning he felt ill probably looked like this.

For several minutes he scanned the slide. There were plenty of roundish red cells. There were a few irregularly shaped white cells. But no definite sign of malaria—or of yellow fever. The trouble was, that didn't prove a thing. Diagnosing illness with a microscope was often difficult. Sometimes yellow fever patients had fewer white cells in their blood. But often yellow fever blood looked pretty normal. And malaria? That was tricky, too. Sometimes it was hard to see the tiny organisms that caused the illness in a single drop of blood.

Clearly, the microscope wasn't going to provide a simple answer. And as James Carroll looked up from the eyepiece, he must have known that there was nothing else to do but wait.

If it was malaria, he'd know it soon. There would be violent, periodic fevers, vomiting, sores around his lips, and soaking sweats. And if it was yellow fever, well, he'd recognize the bloodshot eyes, the bleeding nose and gums, and the awful yellow skin. One way or another, he'd find out about his illness soon enough.

Nobody knows how long Carroll sat in front of his microscope that

37

morning. But he was still there when Lazear and Agramonte walked through the laboratory door—and stared. Carroll looked awful. His face was flushed; his eyes were red. But he tried to joke. The illness was nothing, he said. He'd just somehow "caught cold."

Both doctors begged him to go to bed. Carroll, however, was a stubborn man. As a youngster he'd struggled against poverty. He'd fought to go to medical school. He was used to hardships, and he wasn't the sort who'd let a little bout of sickness beat him down. Still, finally, he agreed to stretch out on a sofa.

It didn't help. By afternoon, James Carroll was lying in the hospital. At seven p.m. his temperature had reached 102. Soon there was no question

Microscopic view of the one-celled organism that causes malaria (the dark patch) among blood cells.
This is what Dr. Carroll probably expected to see in his blood when he became sick.

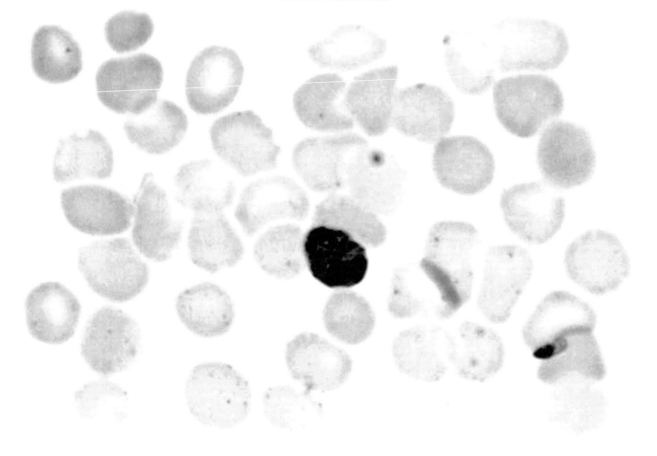

about the diagnosis: the scientist had come down with yellow fever.

But how could he have gotten the disease? In a state bordering on panic, Lazear and Agramonte reviewed the possibilities.

Could it have happened when Carroll visited the autopsy room at Las Animas Hospital in Havana a few days earlier? Could that be where he'd picked up the infection?

Or had it happened in the Camp Columbia lab when Carroll let Lazear's enfeebled little insect bite his arm?

Both doctors knew that there was only one good way to find an answer. They would have to let the mosquito that bit Carroll bite another person. Then they would have to see if that victim developed a clear-cut case of the disease.

The experiment was basically simple. But to do it, they had to have a healthy volunteer.

Agramonte wasn't a good candidate. There was a chance he'd had a very mild case of yellow fever while growing up in Cuba and now might be completely immune to the disease.

Lazear wasn't a great choice either. He'd already been bitten several times by mosquitoes that had previously bitten yellow fever patients. Since those bites hadn't made him sick, there was a chance he, too, might actually be immune to the disease.

A fresh volunteer would be best.

The scientists had barely come to that conclusion when Private William Dean walked by the lab and happened to look in.

Dean, a young unmarried man, had just arrived in Cuba. He'd never been near Carroll or any other yellow fever victims, but he had certainly heard a lot about the team's experiments.

"You still fooling with mosquitoes, Doctor?" Dean asked, as he stood in the doorway.

"Yes," said Lazear. "Will you take a bite?"

"Sure. I ain't scared of 'em," Dean replied.

39

Lazear looked at Agramonte. Agramonte nodded. The young private seemed to be the perfect volunteer.

Dr. Lazear picked up the tube containing the mosquito that had bitten Carroll. He inverted the tube, pulled out the cotton plug, and placed the opening flat against Dean's bare arm. The bug flew down, and all three men waited while it settled on the soldier's skin, inserted its proboscis, and sucked blood.

For the next few days, Lazear and Agramonte didn't tell anyone at Camp Columbia about Carroll's mosquito bite or Dean's. Instead, they tried to work. They worried about Carroll, and they wondered privately if young Dean was going to get sick.

Carroll himself lay in the hospital, fighting the disease. Roger Ames, the army doctor with the most experience in treating yellow fever, monitored the patient and saw the scientist's temperature rise to 104. He watched as Dr. Carroll's skin and bloodshot eyes turned lemon yellow. The sick man's pulse was slow. His condition was definitely critical, but there was very little Dr. Ames could do. Available drugs like quinine, castor oil, mercury compounds, and opium had no effect on yellow fever. To combat the disease, Ames ordered nurses to keep the patient quiet. He made sure that Dr. Carroll ate nothing while the fever soared but insisted that the scientist sip lemonade or water every hour.

At one point Carroll felt a sharp pain in his chest that seemed to stop his heart. Sometimes he babbled feverishly. But experiments were often on his mind. Once, when he ordered his nurse, Ms. Warner, to give the lab mosquitoes a meal of ripe banana, she obligingly obeyed. But when Dr. Carroll said that a mosquito bite had caused his illness, Nurse Warner was seriously shocked. A mosquito causing yellow fever? Why, everybody knew that Finlay's theory was a joke. The whole idea was crazy, and, before she went off duty, Ms. Warner had formed her own opinion of the sick man's silly statement. "Patient delirious," she noted briefly on the chart.

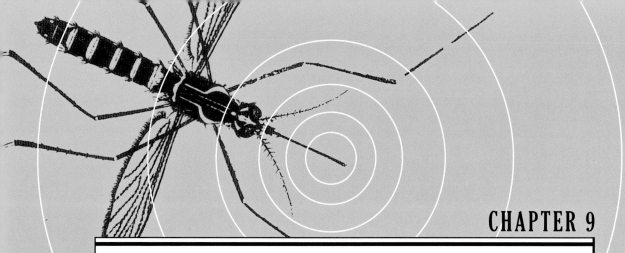

CHAPTER 9

"DID THE MOSQUITO DO IT?"

September 5–8, 1900

The situation was serious. Carroll was desperately ill. Lazear and Agramonte were waiting to see if Dean would come down with yellow fever. And Reed, far away in Washington, D.C., could only wait for bulletins and wonder. Was Carroll's attack simply a tragic accident? Or was it an important clue—a clue that would finally crack the yellow fever mystery? Upset and distracted, Reed poured out his feelings in a letter to his old friend Major Jefferson Kean. "I cannot begin to describe my mental distress and depression over this most unfortunate turn of affairs," Reed wrote. To Reed, Carroll's illness was terrible. It was worrying. But, from a scientific point of view, it was also fascinating. And the team's chief investigator desperately wanted to know how Carroll had gotten sick. "Can it be that [the mosquito] was the source of infection?" he asked Kean.

As the days went by, Reed got reports from Camp Columbia. For the most part, the word was grim. Carroll was suffering from violent headaches. Light hurt his eyes. The attack was severe. The fever was

41

Record of Variations of Temperature beginning _____

3—787

NAME.		COMPANY.	REGIMENT.	NATIVITY.
James Carroll		4 a Surgeon U.S.A.	England	

Day of Month.	Aug 31st	Sept 1st	Sept 2nd "	3rd " " "	4 " " "	5th "

Temperature chart (107° to 95°) with plotted temperature curve across the days, with Time of Day, Morn./Even. columns.

Pulse.						
Respiration.						

Medical Officers are requested to exercise the greatest care and thoroughness in preparing the clinical histories of the medical and surgical history of the present war. Whenever possible the text should be illustrated by sketches, drawin writing space under any of the headings be insufficient to give the necessary information, this should be supplied by a belongs. The writing must be plain and in ink.

Accurate information on the effects of the modern bullet is especially desirable. In the clinical study of this subject described, the track of the bullet marked on the outline figures of the "Surgical Report" and the effects on bones, joints, a the degree of shock should be carefully estimated and accurately recorded. The remote results of gunshot wounds des termination of the case the report should be promptly made out and forwarded to the Surgeon General.

Record of urine Passed
each 24 hours.

42

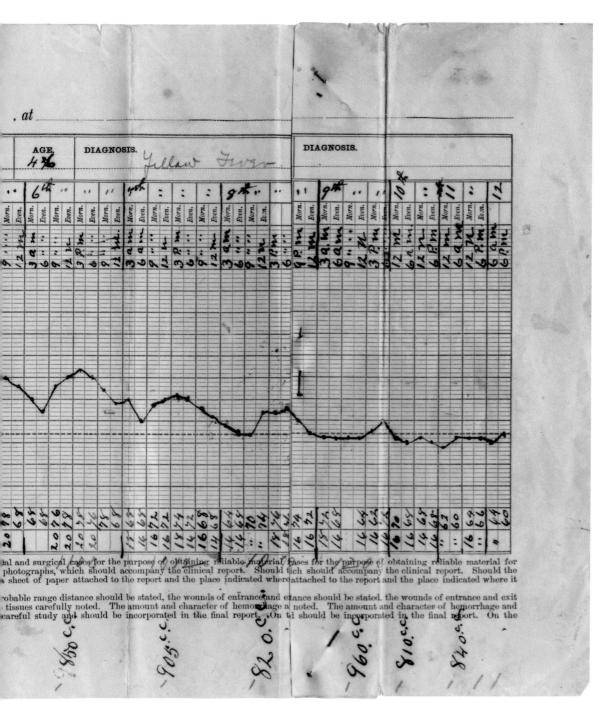

Dr. Carroll's fever chart. This record shows his temperature, pulse, and rate of breathing during his attack of yellow fever.

Walter Reed and his teenage daughter, Blossom. While Carroll was ill,
Reed was home in the United States with his family.

high. For several days it seemed Carroll might die. Then suddenly on September 7, there was wonderful news. For the first time in a week the sick man's temperature was normal. The outlook for recovery was good, and Reed immediately dashed off a note:

> My Dear Carroll:
>   Hip Hip Hurrah . . .
>   Really I can never recall such a sense of relief in all my life, as the news of your recovery gives me . . . .
>   God bless you, my boy.

Then on the back of the envelope Reed scribbled: "Did the Mosquito Do It?"

It was the big question. And—though Reed didn't know it when he wrote that note—Lazear and Agramonte already had a clue.

On September 5, about a week after he had been bitten by the mosquito, Private Dean didn't feel well.

At first the soldier was just a little weary and lightheaded. Then his eyes became bloodshot. His face flushed red, and his temperature soared. Soon Private Dean was in the hospital. It seemed that the mosquito that had bitten Carroll had caused another case of yellow fever.

In the hospital, Dean suffered through a mild case of the disease. Carroll slowly started to recover, and Jesse Lazear was excited. On September 8 he sat down and sent his wife the latest news. "I rather think I am on the track of the real germ," he wrote, "but nothing must be said as yet, not . . . a hint. I have not mentioned it to a soul."

Private William Dean's fever chart. The graph shows that Dean's temperature went down quickly and that his attack of yellow fever was not as severe as Carroll's.

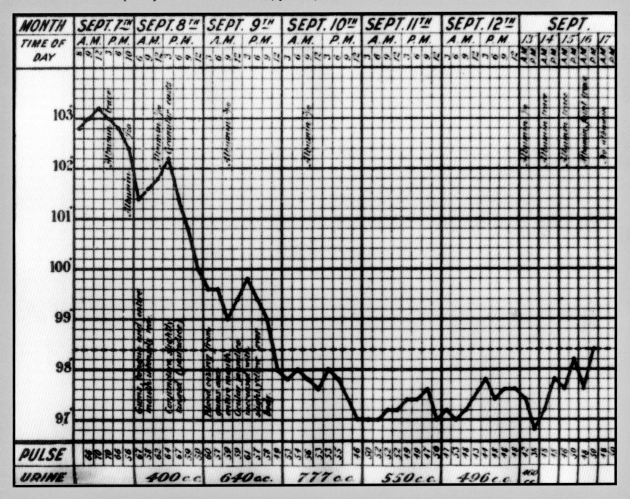

CHAPTER 10

"DOCTOR, ARE YOU SICK?"

September 9–26, 1900

In September an epidemic of yellow fever broke out in Havana. The hospitals admitted two hundred and sixty-nine cases, and one out of every five patients died. It was more important than ever to find a solution to the yellow fever problem, but manpower was in short supply. Carroll was still so weak from his attack that he couldn't stand or change position without help. Agramonte was getting ready to return to the United States for a brief vacation. Reed was still in Washington, putting the finishing touches on his report.

In Cuba, however, Jesse Lazear was working hard. Day after day he tended the insects, carried out experiments, and jotted down his records in a big lab notebook and another smaller book he carried in the pocket of his shirt. At last the work seemed to be paying off. The results looked promising. Both Carroll and Dean had developed yellow fever after mosquito bites. The trouble was, Lazear couldn't be absolutely certain that Carroll's case hadn't been an accident. He couldn't be one hundred percent sure that Carroll hadn't gotten yellow fever from another source. And there were other questions, too. Why, for instance, had Carroll and Dean become sick when other people bitten by "infected" mosquitoes had managed to stay healthy? Was there something different or special about the insects that had bitten those two men? To make a breakthrough, Lazear would have to be able to answer all those questions. He'd need to know exactly how and when a mosquito could transmit the yellow fever germ—and he'd need to prove it beyond the slightest doubt. There were lots of experiments he had to do. And Jesse Lazear was doing them when, on September 13, he was bitten by a mosquito.

No one ever knew exactly how it happened. Later, Lazear said that the incident had taken place at Las Animas Hospital in Havana. He was holding a

This picture, taken in Cuba before the Reed team began work, shows Dr. Lazear holding his son, Houston, as the child's nanny stands by. Another child, a daughter, was born in the United States while Lazear was doing yellow fever research.

test tube containing a mosquito against a patient's belly when a wild mosquito flew down and landed on his hand. The whole thing was an accident, he said.

And maybe that was true.

But if that was how it happened, then why did Jesse Lazear write a mysterious note in the team's lab notebook on September 13, 1900? Why did he write the following?

Guinea pig No. 1—red
Sep. 13 This guinea pig bitten today by a mosquito which developed from egg laid by a mosquito which bit Tanner—8/6.
This mosquito bit Suarez 8/30
Hernandez 9/2
De Long 9/7
Fernandez 9/10

And who—or what—was "Guinea pig No. 1"?

It wasn't a four-footed animal; that much was plain. Lazear didn't use guinea pigs in his experiments because they were immune from yellow fever. No healthy human volunteer ever claimed to have been bitten in a mosquito experiment that day. In fact, the only healthy person who seemed to have been bitten on September 13 was Dr. J. Lazear himself.

So was "Guinea pig No. 1" actually Lazear? Did Dr. Lazear deliberately let an infected mosquito bite him? And, if his bite was really part of an experiment, why did he tell a tale about a wild mosquito? Why didn't he identify himself as "Guinea pig No. 1"?

Did he lie because his family might disapprove of such a dangerous experiment?

Did he think his life insurance company would cancel out his policy if he admitted that he'd dared to take a deadly risk?

Nobody will probably ever know the answers. But the results of that

mosquito "accident" were immediate and clear. Five days later, on the morning of September 18, Jesse Lazear just didn't feel well. At six p.m. the doctor had a chill. Later that same evening, Private John Kissinger found the scientist sitting at his desk and busily writing up his research notes. To Kissinger, Lazear seemed "nervous." The doctor's face looked "flushed," and his eyes were red.

"Doctor, are you sick?" the soldier asked.

"Yes, Kissinger, I do feel sick."

"Have you reported to Dr. [Ames]?"

"No, Kissinger," Lazear replied, and kept on working.

By midnight, Lazear must have wanted to lie down, but it was morning before he had all the facts on paper. By then he was much too sick to struggle. At eleven a.m. Dr. Jesse Lazear was carried to the hospital on a stretcher. His temperature was high, and he told the attending nurse that he had yellow fever.

Two days later, his temperature had risen to 104. His attack was clearly worse than Carroll's, but Lazear was young. He was strong. There was still a good chance that he might recover.

Reed, far away in Washington, tried to be optimistic. "I can but believe Lazear will pull through," he wrote to Carroll. "I hope & pray that he does." But Carroll, who stopped by to visit, was alarmed. As he sat beside the hospital bed, the older scientist saw a flash of panic in Lazear's eyes. Then, suddenly the sick man's belly heaved and a stream of thick black vomit shot out of his mouth. It was the worst possible sign, and both Carroll and Lazear knew that patients who vomited black, partially digested blood usually died of yellow fever.

For the next day or so, Lazear's temperature stayed high. Frantic with delirium, he leaped out of bed and raced around his hospital room until two female nurses and a hospital corpsman forced him back onto his cot.

On September 24, a nurse noted that Dr. Lazear's temperature was getting lower. By morning on September 25, it hovered just below 100. Then, late that afternoon, the doctor's pulse began to quicken. His breath began to come in desperate pants. By 8:45 that evening, it was over. At age thirty-four, the scientist had died of yellow fever.

On the following day, friends, officers from headquarters, and all the members of the Camp Columbia medical staff turned out to watch as Dr. Lazear was buried in a flag-draped coffin with full military honors.

On that same day, far away in Massachusetts, Mabel Lazear, the doctor's wife and the mother of their two small children, opened a telegram and stared at seven terrible words scrawled on the printed form: "Dr. Lazear died at 8 this evening."

The news was cruel. It was also particularly shocking because no one had ever told Mrs. Lazear that her husband had been taken sick.

Coffins of U.S. soldiers killed in 1898 during the Spanish-American War. Dr. Lazear, who sacrificed his life in the war against yellow fever, was given a soldier's funeral and buried in a flag-draped coffin that probably looked like one of these.

CHAPTER 11

SORTING IT OUT

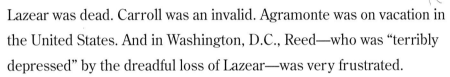

September 27–November 2, 1900

Lazear was dead. Carroll was an invalid. Agramonte was on vacation in the United States. And in Washington, D.C., Reed—who was "terribly depressed" by the dreadful loss of Lazear—was very frustrated.

Three men—Lazear, Carroll, and Dean—had been bitten by mosquitoes. Each had developed yellow fever; but, as Reed pointed out in a letter he wrote to Carroll, the first two cases didn't *"prove"* that infected bugs had actually caused the illness. Lazear *might* have picked up yellow fever from the patients he was seeing at Las Animas Hospital. Carroll *might* have been infected by the remains of yellow fever victims when he visited the autopsy lab. That left the third case: Dean.

As far as anyone knew, the young soldier couldn't have gotten yellow fever from anything except the mosquito. He definitely hadn't been in contact with yellow fever victims before his bite. But what about the few days afterward? Had Dean come close to any yellow fever patients or the remains of yellow fever victims between the time that he'd been bitten and the time he'd gotten sick? Had he been in Havana, where the disease was raging? Was there anything except the mosquito that could possibly have given him the illness?

Reed had to find out; and, a few days after Lazear's death, he headed back to Cuba. This time the sea voyage was pleasant, and Reed was soon greeting James Carroll and the rest of the medical staff at Camp Columbia.

Although it had been about a month since Carroll's illness, the bacteriologist was still feeble and unwell. There was no chance he'd be able to do much work, and Reed promptly ordered his colleague to go back home to the United States for a rest. Agramonte was still away, so Reed plunged into the work on his own—and one of the first items on his agenda was investigating the interesting case of Private Dean.

On one October day he met Dean on the patio outside the Officers' Quarters. There, according to one of the young doctors who was stationed at Camp Columbia, the two men held the following discussion.

"My man," Reed said, "I am studying your case of yellow fever and I want to ask you a few questions." Then, to test Dean's honesty, Reed held up a coin. "I will give you this ten dollar gold piece if you will

Dr. Walter Reed aboard ship during one of his trips to Cuba.

say you were off this [base] at any time . . . until you returned sick with yellow fever," he told the soldier.

Dean probably could have used the money, but he apparently wasn't interested in telling lies.

"I'm sorry, sir," the private replied truthfully, "but I did not leave the post at any time during that period."

That was exactly what Reed had been hoping to hear. If Dean truly hadn't left Camp Columbia before or after his mosquito bite, there was no way he could have been exposed to the yellow fever epidemic in Havana. There was no way he could have had contact with the patients in the military yellow fever ward just outside the army base. As far as Reed could tell, young Dean had never been close to any yellow fever victims. It seemed that the mosquito really had given Private Dean a case of the disease.

But Reed was still cautious. He told Dean to sit down and tell him the whole story of his experiences. When the young man finished, Reed was impressed. Dean seemed honest. The case looked watertight; still, Reed had lots of questions. Why, for instance, if a mosquito bite had caused Dean's attack, had Dr. Carlos Finlay failed to produce a batch of yellow fever cases when he'd let infected bugs bite humans? Why had some of Lazear's volunteers stayed healthy when they were bitten by infected bugs? *Why did some bites from infected insects cause the disease when others didn't?*

Sitting at the long wooden table in his quarters, Reed plowed through material and tried to find an explanation. He went through Lazear's painstaking notes on the experiments. He read and reviewed scientific articles. Carefully, he counted the days between the time the mosquitoes were infected and the time they seemed to be able to pass the disease to others. Carroll, he noticed, had been bitten by a mosquito that had been infected twelve days before it bit him, while the mosquito that bit Dean had been infected sixteen days before his bite. That was interesting. And, Reed noted, it fit in with other facts. Recently, a scientific article had stated that there was always a space of about fourteen days between the appearance of the first group of cases and the appearance of the second group in yellow fever outbreaks.

Twelve days. Fourteen days. Sixteen days. The numbers whirled around Reed's brain, and gradually the data began to make some sense.

There seemed to be a reason that some mosquito bites produced yellow fever and some did not. And perhaps that reason was timing.

To Reed it seemed that after a mosquito sucked in yellow fever germs, those germs had to stay in the mosquito's body for *at least* twelve days before the insect could pass the illness to another victim.

If Reed was right, then Dr. Finlay's earlier experiments had failed probably because the Cuban scientist hadn't let the yellow fever germs remain inside his insects long enough. And Lazear's early experiments? Well, they too hadn't succeeded probably for that reason.

By the middle of October, Reed was pretty sure that he was onto something. But in science "pretty sure" isn't good enough. If Reed was going to prove absolutely that mosquitoes carried yellow fever, if he was going to demonstrate exactly how the insects did it, he was going to have to confirm his hunches with experiments. And experiments cost money.

On the morning of October 12, Reed climbed into a carriage and headed to Havana for an appointment with Major General Leonard Wood, the governor-general of Cuba. As the two men stood by a window that looked out toward the bustling Cuban harbor, Reed came directly to the point. "General Wood," he said, "will you give me $10,000 to continue and complete these [yellow fever] experiments?"

General Wood had started his military career as an army doctor. He understood that the team's work was important, and he answered very quickly. "I will give you $10,000, and if that proves insufficient, I will give you $10,000 more."

The sum of ten thousand dollars in 1900 was roughly equivalent to
54   two hundred and fifty thousand dollars in today's money. It was a huge

commitment, and to celebrate, Reed went out to lunch with his old friend Jefferson Kean, the chief U.S. medical officer for western Cuba. Together the two men drank a toast to success with a bottle of red wine. Then it was back to work—and Reed was busy.

He couldn't yet prove that yellow fever was *always* caused by a mosquito bite, but he could tell the scientific world that in one case—Dean's—a mosquito bite had caused a single, clear-cut attack of yellow fever. And that was big news. It was news that could make scientific history. Most important, it was news that might save lives—and Reed wanted to present it at once.

In the space of eight days Reed wrote a five-thousand-word report stating that his team had found evidence that clearly indicated that the bite of a

The governor-general of Cuba, Leonard Wood, a former army doctor and friend of Theodore Roosevelt's, enthusiastically supported the Reed team's work.

mosquito could cause a case of yellow fever. Then he packed his bags and boarded a ship headed for the United States. When the ship docked, he traveled west, and at three thirty on the afternoon of October 23, 1900, Major Walter Reed stepped up to the podium in an Indianapolis lecture room and began to read his report to the members of the American Public Health Association.

First, Reed thanked Dr. Finlay for suggesting the mosquito theory and for providing the mosquito eggs that the team had used for research. He carefully described the team's experiments. Then, finally, he read the most important words:

> From our study thus far of yellow fever, we draw the following conclusions:
> 1. Bacillus icteroides stands in no causative relation to yellow fever. . . .
> 2. The mosquito serves as the intermediate host [the carrier] for the . . . [germ] of yellow fever.

It was an exciting, groundbreaking statement, but not everyone believed it. The *Philadelphia Medical Journal* called Reed's report "pure speculation." The *Washington Post* just scoffed. In an article on November 2, 1900, the *Post* said:

> Of all the silly and nonsensical rigmarole about yellow fever . . . the silliest beyond compare is to be found in the arguments . . . engendered by the mosquito hypothesis [theory].

The trouble was that Reed didn't have much evidence. At the moment he could show that one single case of yellow fever had been caused by a mosquito. But a single case didn't *prove* anything. It could be an accident, a fluke. And good scientists believed only facts that had been tested and proved time after time in carefully set-up experiments.

If Walter Reed was going to convince the scientific world that mosquitoes were the cause of yellow fever, he clearly had a lot more research work to do.

CHAPTER 12

PROBLEMS

November 1900

As soon as he returned to Cuba at the beginning of November, Walter Reed started to use the ten thousand dollars that General Wood had provided to make arrangements for a brand-new series of experiments.

The first job was setting up a new camp where the team could carry out the tests, and Reed knew exactly how he wanted it to be constructed. The new camp had to be built on a site that had absolutely no mosquitoes. It had to be located in a place that had never been inhabited by yellow fever patients. And it had to be set up in a lonesome, isolated area—an area that strangers (who might be carrying the yellow fever germ) weren't likely to visit.

Of course, that list of requirements sounded picky. But each of those conditions was important. Each was designed to guarantee that there would be no accidental cases of yellow fever in the new station. To prove that mosquitoes carried yellow fever, Reed knew that he would have to show that each case of the disease in the new camp was deliberately caused by the team's own insect experiments and not by some chance infection or contamination.

Dr. Agramonte had just returned from his vacation; and, at Reed's request, the Spanish-speaking scientist took charge of searching for a campsite. After scouting the countryside around Camp Columbia, he found a bare, isolated two-acre patch of land that the team could rent for twenty dollars a month. It was a dry, wind-blown place where mosquitoes didn't live or breed. It had never been inhabited by yellow fever victims, and it seemed perfect. Reed drew up plans. Workers started to put up tents and buildings on the spot, and someone named the brand-new station Camp Lazear in honor of the scientists' dead colleague.

But that was only the beginning.

While workers hammered nails at the new campsite, Reed focused his mind on other problems. And one of the biggest was mosquitoes.

Keeping the insects alive had always been difficult. Now it was harder than ever. The autumn months brought cooler weather. The lower temperatures killed mosquitoes. And while Reed was struggling to keep a few bugs alive for his experiments, a huge tropical storm hit the island of Cuba. Gale-force winds knocked over trees. Rain poured down. Temperatures plummeted into the low sixties. And, when Reed walked into the officers' mess hall for lunch on November 15, he told the other Camp Columbia doctors that there was bad news. Most of the laboratory mosquitoes that Lazear had raised from Finlay's eggs had died of the cold. Worst of all, there were very few dried mosquito eggs left. Work on the new experiments would have to stop until the team could

The tents used to house volunteers and medical personnel at Camp Lazear, the site where the Reed team performed its most important experiments.

Modern photo of a ladle of water containing mosquito eggs and larvae (immature mosquitoes). In 1900, when billions of mosquitoes swarmed through Cuba, sights such as this were common.

breed more bugs. That could take weeks, and Reed sounded so upset that the other Camp Columbia doctors tried to cheer him up. The weather was sure to get warmer, they told him. There were lots of mosquitoes left in Cuba. And to prove that point a bunch of young doctors left the mess hall and went bug hunting in a nearby dump. There, among the piles of rusty old containers, they saw a flock of striped *Aedes aegypti* mosquitoes buzzing around a can. The can was full of water, and floating in that water were enough mosquito eggs and mosquito larvae (immature mosquitoes) to keep the team supplied for months.

That was one piece of good news. Then, around the middle of November, there was another. James Carroll returned from sick leave. He still wasn't one hundred percent healthy, but he immediately pitched in by helping to raise, infect, and keep records of the mosquitoes that were going to be used in the new series of experiments.

Things were going well, but the team still had to face one enormously important problem: Where were the scientists going to find volunteers who were willing to take part in the new experimental tests?

To present a watertight case, the team had to show that the mosquito hypothesis was true and that all the other old ideas about the cause of yellow fever were completely false. With the help of his colleagues, Reed had already proved that *Bacillus icteroides* didn't cause the illness. Now the team needed to deal with the last two remaining theories. First, they had to prove once and for all that infected mosquitoes *did* cause yellow fever. And, second, they needed to show that being in contact with infected clothing and bedding was definitely not the cause of the disease. To do that, they needed two sets of human volunteers for a series of experiments. The first set would have to spend several weeks wearing and using clothing and sheets that had been stained by the sweat, vomit, urine, and feces of yellow fever patients. The second set would have to do what Carroll, Dean, and Lazear had done. They would have to be bitten by infected mosquitoes.

But how many normal, healthy, sensible people would volunteer for such disgusting and dangerous experiments?

Of course, Reed could order soldiers to take part in the tests without telling them about the dangers or asking their permission. In 1900 scientists sometimes did something that is now illegal in the United States and many other countries. They sometimes dosed unsuspecting patients with disease

A highly magnified modern photo of a fish about to eat a tiny immature mosquito. Mosquitoes live in water before they become adults. In very warm weather, it may take a mosquito egg a week to develop into a mature insect; in cold weather, it may take almost a month. By eating large quantities of immature mosquitoes (larvae), fish (like the one in this photo) help to keep down the number of these insect pests.

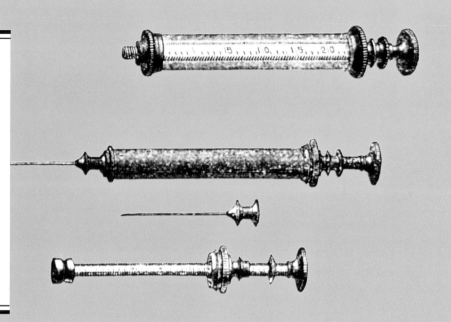

Syringes similar to those used in Walter Reed's time. In 1900 syringes like these were sometimes used to inject germs and untested drugs into unsuspecting patients. Dr. Giuseppe Sanarelli, for example, injected Bacillus icteroides *into five patients without asking for their consent.*

germs or untested drugs without bothering to explain the risks or to ask these victims for consent. But Reed refused to do that. Like William Osler, the famous nineteenth-century doctor and professor of medicine, Walter Reed thought that "deliberately injecting a poison . . . into a human being, unless you obtain that man's sanction [permission], is . . . criminal."

If Reed was going to do yellow fever experiments, he wanted to be honest and up-front about it. He wanted volunteers to know they were risking sickness and death by participating. What's more, he wanted to do something new—something that scientists hadn't done before. Because he felt his yellow fever insect experiments were extremely dangerous, Reed wanted each and every volunteer to sign a consent form indicating in writing that he or she was willing to undertake the experiment and truly understood the hazards.

The question was, would Reed find anyone brave enough to sign up? 61

CHAPTER 13

"WE ARE DOING IT FOR MEDICAL SCIENCE"

November 1900

As the days went by, Reed and his team began looking for volunteers. Candidates had to be young and healthy—because young, healthy people had the best chance of surviving yellow fever. They had to be single, so that their sickness or death would not injure an entire family. And, of course, they had to be willing to risk getting the disease.

The truth, however, was that yellow fever was so common in Cuba that anyone who set foot on the island and hadn't previously had the illness was likely to come down with it anyway. And that piece of information gave the Reed team an idea.

Immigrants from Spain were landing in Cuba all the time. Many were young, healthy, and single. All of them knew that they might get yellow fever in Cuba. And, maybe, the team thought, since these newcomers were already running the risk of getting the disease naturally, some of them would be willing to volunteer for the experiments.

With Reed's permission, Agramonte interviewed a group of recent immigrants and carefully explained the requirements and terms. Each volunteer who signed Reed's consent form and agreed to be bitten by mosquitoes would be paid $100 (the equivalent of about $2,400 in today's money). In addition, those who came down with yellow fever would receive an extra $100 and the very best medical care the U.S. Army team could possibly provide. By the time Agramonte had finished, four Spanish men—Antonio Benigno, Nicanor Fernandez, Becente Presedo, and José Martinez—had agreed to volunteer and had signed a consent form written in English and Spanish.

It was a start. And Agramonte wasn't the only recruiter.

One afternoon, medical officer Dr. Roger Ames saw a twenty-four-year-old civilian clerk named John Moran walking across the Camp Columbia parade ground. When Moran stopped to chat, Ames told the young man that Reed was offering money to anyone who'd volunteer for the new series of experiments. Was Moran interested in signing up?

Like everyone else at Camp Columbia, Moran knew that Dr. Jesse Lazear had died of yellow fever. He knew that the disease had just about killed Carroll. But young John Moran badly wanted to become a doctor. He needed a lot of money to pay for medical school. When Ames spoke, Moran later wrote in his memoirs, the first idea that popped into his head was, "Just think, Johnny, what that . . . [amount of money] will mean to you." The offer was tempting. But Moran didn't want to make a snap decision. He told Ames to let him "sleep over it." Then he went back to his quarters to discuss the proposal with his roommate, Private John Kissinger.

At midnight the men were still talking. The danger was clear. The money

The undersigned, Antonio Benino *Antonio Benino*

being more than twenty-five years of age, native of Cerceda,

in the province of   Corima   , the son of Manuel Benino

and Josefa Castro   here states by these presents, being in

the enjoyment and exercise of his own very free will, that he consents

to submit himself to experiments for the purpose of determining the

methods of transmission of yellow fever, made upon his person by the

Commission appointed for this purpose by the Secretary of War of the

United States, and that he gives his consent to undergo the said ex-

periments for the reasons and under the conditions below stated.

The undersigned understands perfectly well that in case of the

development of yellow fever in him, that he endangers his life to a

certain extent but it being entirely impossible for him to avoid the

infection during his stay in this island, he prefers to take the

chance of contracting it intentionally in the belief that he will

receive from the said Commission the greatest care and the most skill-

ful medical service.

It is understood that at the completion of these experiments, with-

in two months from this date, the undersigned will receive the sum of

$100 in American gold and that in case of his contracting yellow fever

at any time during his residence in this camp, he will receive in addi-

tion to that sum a further sum of $100 in American gold, upon his re-

covery and that in case of his death because of this disease, the

Commission will transmit the said sum (two hundred American dollars)

to the person whom the undersigned shall designate at his convenience.

The undersigned binds himself not to leave the bounds of this camp

during the period of the experiments and will forfeit all right to the

benefits named in this contract if he breaks this agreement.

And to bind himself he signs this paper in duplicate, in the Experi-

mental Camp, near Quemados, Cuba, on the 26th day of November

nineteen hundred.

                                        The contracting party,
On the part of the Commission:
                                          Antonio Benigno
     Walter Reed
     Maj. & Surg., U.S.A.

64   *An English translation of the consent form stating the volunteer Antonio Benigno*
      (misspelled as "Benino") was willing to participate in the mosquito experiments.

was attractive. But that wasn't all. As the night wore on, Moran got more and more excited about being part of the experiments. Signing up was more than just a fast way to make some cash. It was a chance to help save lives. A chance to help make medical history. In fact, getting involved in the fight to conquer yellow fever seemed so important that Moran decided to refuse the money. He was going to take part in the experiments solely for the sake of helping science.

Dr. Roger P. Ames. Dr. Ames, who was considered an expert at treating yellow fever, took care of patients who came down with the disease at Camp Columbia and Camp Lazear.

"[Don't be] a fool," Kissinger told him. But Moran had made up his mind. He was positive. Finally, even Kissinger was convinced. "Whatever you do, John, I am with you," Kissinger said. "We'll volunteer together."

The next morning, the two men went to Reed's room in the Officers' Quarters. The door was open. "Good morning," Reed said. "What can I do for you?" For a minute Moran struggled for words. Then the young man poured out the story. He and Kissinger were volunteering, Moran told Reed, "without the bonus or money award which [the army was] offering. . . . We are doing it," Moran said, "for medical science."

Now, some people say that Reed turned to the two volunteers and said, "I take my hat off to you, gentlemen." And some people claim that Reed said simply, "I salute you." But Moran wrote in his memoir that Reed just "gladly accepted" with "a gleam in his eyes . . . of pleasure and satisfaction."

Later, however, the major voiced his actual feelings. Those who volunteered for the experiments, Reed said, showed a type of "courage [that] has never been surpassed in the annals of the Army of the United States."

That was high praise, and soon many men deserved it. In the weeks that followed, fifteen other Americans signed up for the experiments. Although many agreed to accept money for their participation, at least one other man refused the reward and agreed to take part solely for the sake of science.

The volunteer problem had been solved more easily than Reed could have expected, and it was time for the real scientific work to start.

Members of the Hospital Corps at Camp Columbia. Many of Reed's volunteers came from this group. John Kissinger is number 10. (Other volunteers are identified in the Appendix.)

CHAPTER 14

TESTING TIMES

November–December 1900

On November 20, 1900, Camp Lazear officially opened. Volunteers and other personnel were housed in seven newly erected tents. Two specially constructed small wooden buildings were ready to be used for the experiments, and a barbed-wire fence kept out unwanted visitors.

To make sure all the men in his experimental group were healthy, Reed ordered medics to take the volunteers' pulse and temperature three times a day. There were going to be no slip-ups, no accidental illnesses, nothing that would allow critics to find fault with the experiments—not if Reed could help it. Everything seemed to be in place, but Reed still had a nagging worry. He knew he'd made sure that his volunteers were young and healthy enough to have a good chance of surviving yellow fever. He knew the men who were volunteering understood the risks. He'd made sure that any volunteer who got the disease would have the best possible medical care. But what if the worst happened? What if one of the volunteers died during the experiments?

67

If that happened, Reed wrote his boss, Army Surgeon General George Sternberg, "I shall regret that I ever undertook this work. The responsibility for the life of a human being weighs upon me very heavily."

Still, thousands of people in Cuba, Africa, and the Americas were dying of yellow fever every year. If the team failed the find the cause, the vicious disease would undoubtedly kill thousands more. Somehow, Reed had to take the necessary steps to find an answer; and on Friday evening, November 30, experiments in Building 1, the "infected clothing" building, got under way.

From the outside the little wooden structure looked like a shack. Its tiny windows were screened and tightly closed to keep out fresh air and mosquitoes. Inside there were three beds, a group of closed boxes, and a stove that heated the place to a germ-friendly temperature of between 90 and 100 degrees. At the entrance stood three American volunteers: Dr. Robert Cooke, Private Warren Jernegan, and Private Levi Folk. As members of the scientific team watched through a window, the three American servicemen entered the building, opened the boxes, and took out nightshirts, underwear, blankets, sheets, and towels that were soiled with the blood, vomit, urine, and feces of yellow fever patients. The stench was terrible. One man threw up, and all three volunteers ran outside gagging.

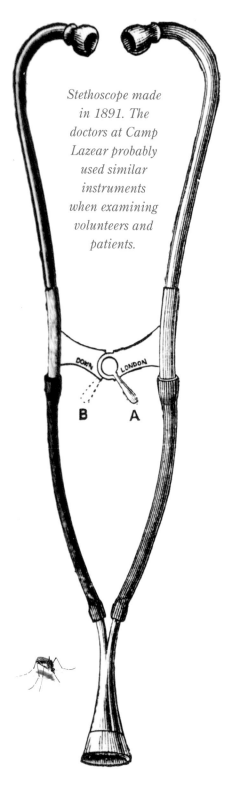

Stethoscope made in 1891. The doctors at Camp Lazear probably used similar instruments when examining volunteers and patients.

Then they went back into the stinking house. They dressed themselves in the filthy clothing, put the dirty sheets and blankets on their beds, waved some of the towels and bedding around to spread the "germs," and slept in the hot, fetid little building for the next twenty nights.

Three weeks later, on December 19, Cooke, Folk, and Jernegan walked out of the "infected clothing building." None of them was sick.

That certainly seemed to show that yellow fever wasn't caused by contact with infected items. But the team wanted to be absolutely sure. To prove that the test results could not have been an accident, they repeated the experiment—twice. Two other groups of men did exactly what Cooke, Folk, and Jernagen had done, and each time the volunteers stayed healthy. That confirmed the findings, and the team knew they'd made real progress. Since starting work, they'd shown that *Bacillus icteroides* and infected clothing didn't have anything to do with the spread of the disease.

But could they prove that infected mosquitoes were the cause of yellow fever?

*The small building in the center was used for the infected clothing
and bedding experiments at Camp Lazear.
"Building 2" was used for the mosquito experiments.*

CHAPTER 15

 MORE BUGS

November–December 1900

Everything was riding on the mosquito work. Almost as soon as Camp Lazear opened, the team began to experiment with bugs.

In November, Private John Kissinger was bitten twice by infected insects. His roommate, John Moran, was also bitten twice. So were several other men. But—although Reed used only mosquitoes that had bitten yellow fever patients at least twelve days before—none of the volunteers ran a temperature. None developed a chill. And none of them showed the slightest sign of yellow fever.

Something was wrong.

Reed, Carroll, and Agramonte anxiously examined the data. Surely, there had to be some logical explanation. But what?

Maybe, Reed thought, the colder fall weather had somehow affected the mosquitoes. Maybe it took longer for the germ to mature inside the insect when temperatures were cool.

Patiently, the scientists adjusted the timing. Then they tried again.

On December 5 at eleven thirty a.m., one of the doctors pressed a glass tube containing an infected mosquito against John Kissinger's arm. After that insect had bitten the young soldier, the doctor repeated the procedure with other infected mosquitoes. By the end of the morning, Kissinger had five itchy bites.

Three days later, Private Kissinger woke a few minutes before midnight feeling, he later said, a little cool. He was just getting up to close the tent flap, when suddenly his body felt like ice. For several long minutes, he huddled, freezing, in his cot. Then, as a little warmth crept back into his limbs, he reached out, lit a candle, and took his temperature. The mercury registered 101. Kissinger quickly sent a guard to fetch the doctor who was sleeping about twenty-five feet

Private John Kissinger, as he looked at the time of the mosquito experiments.

away. Ames arrived in minutes. By then, John Kissinger was in agony. "I felt," he later said, "as though six Ford cars had run over my body. Every bone . . . ached. My spine felt twisted and my head swollen and my eyes felt as if they would pop out of my head, even the ends of my fingers . . . [were] aching."

John Kissinger had yellow fever.

At Reed's request, a panel of distinguished Cuban yellow fever specialists—including Dr. Finlay—examined the young private and confirmed the diagnosis.

For the first time one of the team's mosquito experiments had worked.

In his quarters Reed grabbed a pen and started a letter to his wife. "It is with a great deal of pleasure that I hasten to tell you that we have succeeded in producing an unmistakable case of yellow fever," he started formally. Then all his excitement burst out. "Rejoice with me, sweetheart," he wrote. ". . . I could shout for very joy that heaven has permitted me to establish this. . . . Indeed, my precious heart, you cannot tell what a relief from suspense and anxious waiting this day has been."

It was a big breakthrough. But it was only one experiment. Reed and the rest of the team knew that the results of any one experiment could be an accident. More confirming evidence was needed, and the researchers waited tensely for the next results.

Then, a few days later, Antonio Benigno and two of the other Spanish immigrants who had been bitten by infected mosquitoes became sick. When the panel of experts from Havana examined the patients, the diagnosis was clear. All three Spanish immigrants had come down with yellow fever.

Unidentified man standing beside Building 2, the mosquito building, at Camp Lazear. This building was used for the insect experiments.

The evidence now seemed to show that mosquitoes could carry the illness, but Reed and the team were still not completely satisfied. As Kissinger and the Spaniards slowly recovered, the scientists set out to establish one final and important fact.

For years people had claimed that the yellow fever germ could somehow contaminate whole buildings like a kind of poison gas. The idea was so common that once, in 1898, every building in the Cuban town of Siboney had been burned down to stop a yellow fever epidemic. Now Reed, Carroll, and Agramonte wanted to show that a building could be infected with yellow fever *only* if it contained infected mosquitoes. And that meant doing a new experiment in Building 2, the other wooden building at Camp Lazear.

Inside the little wooden shack was absolutely spic and span. A large wire

73

mesh screen split the room into two parts. Two perfectly clean beds stood on one side of the screen. On the other side was another clean bed and fifteen live, free infected mosquitoes.

At noon on December 21, two male volunteers entered and lay on the beds on the mosquito-free side. John Moran lay undressed on the clean bed in the mosquito area. Within half an hour, he had been bitten by seven bugs. After breaks, during which the participants left the hut, the procedure was repeated one more time that day and again on the next.

By late afternoon on December 22, Moran had fifteen bites and the volunteers on the other side of the screen had none. John Moran then returned to his tent. The two other men slept on the mosquito-free side of the room for the next eighteen nights—breathing the same air that Moran had breathed, being close to the bedding he had touched, and listening to the whine of the mosquitoes on the other side of the screen.

December 23 came. Then December 24. Both Moran and the other "infected mosquito building" volunteers seemed healthy. Then on December 25 at ten

John Moran, as he looked at about the time of the mosquito experiments.

a.m., Moran felt a little strange. He took his temperature, noted that it was 100 degrees, and carefully wrote the figure on his chart. Two hours later, Moran checked again. His fever had climbed to 103. When Christmas dinner was served, Moran went to the mess hall and picked at his turkey, cranberries, and mashed potato. Then he went back to his tent and lay on his cot. Around three in the afternoon, Reed walked in. "Merry Christmas, Moran," he said. "Anything new?" Moran pointed to the temperature chart. Reed checked the figures, looked at Moran's flushed face, put his hand on the young man's forehead—and called an ambulance.

John Moran had joined the list of yellow fever victims.

The two men who had slept on the mosquito-free side of the building remained in perfect health. It was clear—once again—that infected mosquitoes and nothing else caused the disease.

The work was almost done. The experiments had been a success. In the hospital, John Moran was soon on the road to recovery; and, to Reed's immense relief, none of the infected volunteers had died in any of the tests. By the end of December the team had done what they set out to do. They had established that infected mosquitos carried yellow fever. They had proved a theory, and they had also discovered an important way to fight the dreadful sickness. Because scientists now knew that mosquitoes transmitted yellow fever, they also knew that killing mosquitoes would immediately stop the spread of the disease. With

the help of Dr. Finlay and a group of volunteers, the American team had taken a huge step toward conquering a deadly illness.

The culprit: a female Aedes aegypti *mosquito sucking human blood.*

CHAPTER 16

CELEBRATION

Late December 1900

It was time to honor the Cuban scientist who had started it all.

On December 22, Major General Leonard Wood, the governor-general of Cuba, and members of the local medical community gave a huge banquet to honor Dr. Finlay. Reed traveled into Havana for the festivities. Carroll, who was always short of money, didn't go because he couldn't afford a dress uniform. Still, the room at Old Delmonico's Restaurant in Havana was jammed with Cubans and Americans. There were toasts and speeches, handshakes and applause. Dr. Finlay was given a bronze statuette and congratulated in Spanish and in English. For years he'd been laughed at. For years people had said his mosquito theory was a joke. And now—now that a bunch of Americans had proved his hypothesis—Carlos Juan Finlay was the toast of Havana, one of the greatest, most famous men in Cuba.

It was a wonderful, happy time. Everybody seemed to be celebrating, and on Christmas Day two of the officers' wives gave a party at Camp Columbia. Since there weren't many pine trees in Cuba, the women decorated a guava bush. They wrapped up presents. And when Reed opened his, the whole group burst out laughing. The officers' wives had given Major Reed a big wire model of a mosquito, which Reed accepted, he later wrote his wife, "with many blushes."

On December 27 there was another party. This time it was a ball that kept Reed up till one a.m. Then, a few days later, it was December 31, the last New Year's Eve of the nineteenth century.

It was a beautiful, balmy evening. Reed sat at the big table in his quarters, pen in hand. As the hands of the clock moved toward midnight, he wrote to his wife:

> 11:50 p.m. Dec 31, 1900 Only ten minutes of the old century remain, lovie dear. Here I have been reading that most wonderful book—La Roche on Yellow Fever—written in 1853. Forty-seven years later it has been permitted to me and my assistants to lift the impenetrable veil that has surrounded the causation of this most dreadful pest of humanity. . . . The prayer that has been mine for twenty or more years, that I might be permitted in some way or sometime to do something to alleviate human suffering has been answered!

With the help of Dr. Finlay and the team, Reed had done something most people only dream of. He had made a discovery that would save lives, prevent pain, and make the world a better, happier place.

It was a sweet moment.

But it didn't mark a final victory in the war on yellow fever.

Scientists still had to find a cure for the disease. They still needed to track down and isolate the actual germ. And of course there were dozens of

Carlos Finlay became a hero in Cuba. The scientist, who died in 1915, would have been pleased to know that in 1933 the Cuban government issued these stamps in honor of the hundredth anniversary of his birth.

other basic questions still to answer. Why, for instance, had a few volunteers not gotten sick when they were bitten? What happened to the germ inside the insect's body? And could a female mosquito possibly transmit the yellow fever germ to her offspring through her eggs?

Someday, Reed hoped, researchers might find the answers to those questions.

Someday, he hoped, investigators would find the germ, invent a preventative vaccine, and maybe even figure out a cure.

But right now the clocks at Camp Columbia were striking midnight. Outside a corps of army buglers sounded taps to mark the passing of the century. And as Dr. Walter Reed put down his pen, he knew with happy certainty that the first part of one great scientific problem had been solved.

EPILOGUE

After December 31, 1900, the battle against yellow fever continued.

As soon as the results of the Reed team's work were known, public health officials launched an all-out campaign against the mosquitoes that carried the disease. In the United States and Cuba a virtual army of sanitation workers used poison fumes to kill mosquitoes that lurked in buildings and wiped out eggs by spraying oil on the pools, ponds, puddles, and containers of still water where the insects liked to breed. Killing the mosquitoes killed the yellow fever germs the insects carried, and by the end of 1901 there were no cases of the illness in Havana, Cuba. By 1905 the United States was free of the disease. And between 1902 and 1914—thanks to an effective battle against germ-bearing mosquitoes in Central America—U.S. workers were able to safely build the Panama Canal.

As the threat of yellow fever gradually receded, people showered Dr. Finlay and the Reed team scientists with honors, thanks, and praise. Statues of Carlos Finlay were set up in Cuba. A medical society and an American elementary school were named after him; and—though he never won—Dr. Finlay was nominated for one of science's greatest awards, the Nobel Prize in medicine, three times before his death in 1915.

Sanitation worker spraying oil on water to stop mosquitoes from breeding in the early years of the twentieth century. Efforts like this wiped out yellow fever in Cuba, the United States, and parts of Central America by 1914.

Although Walter Reed died of appendicitis in 1902, soon after his return from Cuba, he, too, became a hero. Researchers adopted Reed's belief that all volunteers in scientific experiments should be fully informed of all the risks. In 1909 the American government named the Walter Reed Army Hospital in Washington, D.C., after the team's chief investigator. And in 1929, Congress awarded all the American volunteer scientists (including Dr. Jesse Lazear) one of the nation's highest honors, the Congressional Gold Medal, for their work on yellow fever.

The Congressional Gold Medal
for the conquest of yellow fever. This medal
was awarded to each of the
American scientists and volunteers
who took part in the experiments.
In addition to the medal,
Congress awarded pensions to participants
and decreed that the names
of all the yellow fever scientists and volunteers
be published each year on a
special roll of honor in the Army Register.

But while people and governments were honoring past work on the illness, twentieth-century scientists were looking for new ways to fight the terrible disease. Until his death in 1907, Dr. James Carroll continued to search for the yellow fever germ. Although his efforts were unsuccessful, Carroll ultimately came to believe that the disease is caused by a microbe that is much smaller than bacteria. Dr. Aristides Agramonte, who taught bacteriology in both the United States and Cuba before his death in 1931, tended to agree. And by 1927 scientists knew that the disease was produced by a virus—an extremely tiny, extremely simple microorganism that is so much smaller than bacteria, it cannot be seen with an ordinary microscope.

81

*Scientists infecting white mice with yellow fever. Studying the disease
became easier after researchers learned that white mice could get yellow fever
if the virus was injected directly into their brains.*

Once scientists had identified the virus, the next step was to make a
vaccine that would prevent people from getting the disease. That, however,
proved difficult. Although researchers worked on the problem, progress was
slow until scientists discovered two facts that the Reed team had not known.
In the late 1920s and early 1930s researchers learned that that some types of
monkeys could actually get yellow fever and that, under special conditions, the
virus could sometimes be grown inside the bodies of ordinary white laboratory
mice. Using animals made experimental work much easier; and, finally, in 1936,
Dr. Max Theiler developed a vaccine that safely kept humans from getting the
disease.

Research also continued on other fronts; and, during the twentieth century,
scientists answered many of the questions about the cause and spread of yellow
fever that had puzzled earlier investigators. Researchers learned that an infected

female mosquito can pass the virus on to all her offspring through her eggs. They found that the yellow fever virus actually enters every cell of an infected mosquito's body. And they discovered that a female mosquito transmits the disease by dripping infected saliva into the wound while she is sucking blood.

Additional investigation uncovered more facts, and scientists soon realized that a mosquito must bite a yellow fever patient in the first three days of the illness in order to pick up the infection. They also learned that the virus may have to remain in the insect's body for as much as seventeen days before the bug can infect a person with the disease. To scientists, this information was particularly interesting because it explained why some of the Reed team's volunteers did not come down with yellow fever after being bitten. In some cases, it was clear that the team's mosquitoes weren't carrying the germ because they hadn't bitten yellow fever victims during the crucial three-day infectious period at the beginning of the illness. In other instances, volunteers did not get sick because the germ was not allowed to stay inside the host mosquito long enough.

Today, researchers believe that the yellow fever virus originated in West Africa and was brought to the Americas by slave ships carrying infected

In Africa and South America dense jungles
like this one still harbor mosquitoes that carry the yellow fever virus.

insects. They also know that the germ still lurks in the dense jungles of Africa and South America, where it infects monkeys and is carried by mosquitoes who transmit it to endless generations of offspring through their eggs.

Vaccination programs and mosquito extermination programs have slowed the spread of yellow fever, but it is impossible to completely eliminate the virus. Many poor countries cannot afford to pay for the lifesaving vaccine, and some people now believe that insecticides should not be used to kill mosquitoes because these poisons may damage the environment.

At this moment there is still no cure for yellow fever, and deadly outbreaks of the disease can still occur. In the early 1960s, 30,000 people died during a

Photograph of the yellow fever virus (the small circles) taken with an electron microscope. Viruses are so much smaller than bacteria that they can be seen only with an electron microscope capable of magnifying objects at least 190,000 times.

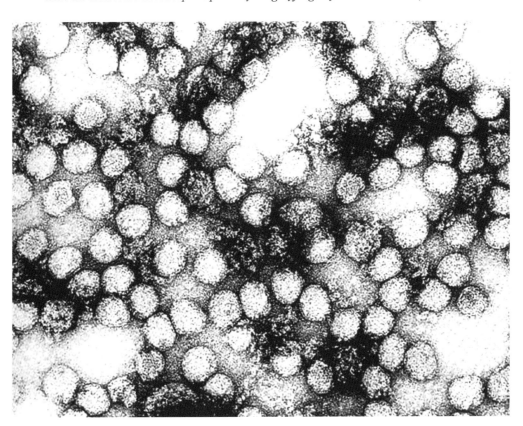

yellow fever epidemic in Ethiopia. The illness continues to plague people in parts of Africa and South America. Only three companies—in France, Brazil, and Senegal—now rank as approved yellow fever vaccine producers and demand is sometimes high. When the government of Paraguay failed to provide enough vaccine during a 2008 outbreak of the fever, desperate people mobbed clinics, yelling, "Vaccinations! Vaccinations!"

In the twenty-first century yellow fever is still one of the many diseases that threaten humans, and doctors are still trying to develop new ways to combat the illness. Some, but not all, modern research can be done with laboratory animals. For that reason, in countries around the world, many scientists and many ordinary people—like those who worked with Reed—are now knowingly risking possible illness, injury, or even death in order to voluntarily participate in experiments that test new vaccines, new treatments, new medical techniques, and new drugs that may one day benefit humanity.

APPENDIX

THE VOLUNTEERS

Unfortunately, little is known about many of the young men who dared to participate in the mosquito experiments, the infected clothing and bedding experiments, or the experiments conducted after December 1900 that involved injecting blood from a yellow fever victim into a healthy volunteer. Lists of the volunteers who took part vary, and some names have probably gone unrecorded. The following partial list does, however, attempt to provide some information about those who were willing to risk their own lives to save others from the scourge of yellow fever.

THE AMERICAN VOLUNTEERS

Andrus, John (1879–1952). Private Andrus served in the army hospital corps and assisted the Reed team by caring for captive mosquitoes. On January 24, 1901, he overheard Reed and Carroll having an argument over whether Reed should offer himself as a volunteer in the yellow fever experiments. Reed was determined to participate. Carroll believed this was ill advised because of the major's age and poor health. Andrus, who feared that if Reed got yellow fever the work would come to a standstill, finally offered to take Reed's place in the experiment. On January 25, 1901, blood from a yellow fever patient was injected into Andrus's body, and, several days later, the private developed the disease. Andrus, who subsequently received the Congressional Gold Medal, later wrote a description of his experiences with the team, which is included in the Philip S. Hench Collection at the University of Virginia. He is #25 in the photo on page 66.

Bullard, John (1872–1944). John Bullard was one of only two civilians who volunteered. He received the Congressional Gold Medal for his participation in the yellow fever experiments.

Cooke, Robert (1874–1943). Dr. Cooke, a physician, was originally stationed at Pinar del Rio. He refused to accept payment for taking part in Reed's tests, but was later given the Congressional Gold Medal for his participation in the "infected clothing and bedding" experiments. He is #4 in the photo on page 66.

Covington, Albert (1877–1934). Private Covington of the Twenty-third Battery, Coast Artillery Corps, was injected with blood from a yellow fever patient and became ill with the disease. He was later awarded the Congressional Gold Medal.

87

Dean, William (1877–1928). Private Dean became sick after being bitten by an infected mosquito on September 6, 1900. His case was the first to truly convince Reed that yellow fever was carried by mosquitoes. He was later given the Congressional Gold Medal for his participation in the experiments (see pp. 39–40, 51–53).

England, Thomas (1876–1943). Private England earned the Congressional Gold Medal because of his participation in the infected clothing and bedding experiments. He is # 24 in the photo on page 66.

Folk, Levi (1870–1936). Private Folk developed yellow fever after being bitten by an infected mosquito in the experiments. He later received the Congressional Gold Medal.

Forbes, Wallace (1878–1948). Private Forbes, a member of the hospital corps, became ill with yellow fever after receiving blood from a victim of the disease. He was later given the Congressional Gold Medal.

Hamann, Paul (1876–1933). Private Hamann became ill with yellow fever after participating in the team's blood inoculation experiments. He received the Congressional Gold Medal.

Hanberry, James (1875–1961). A member of the hospital corps, Private Hanberry participated in the mosquito experiments, became ill with yellow fever, and was later awarded the Congressional Gold Medal.

Hildebrand, James (1862–1935). Private Hildebrand was awarded the Congressional Gold Medal for his role in the yellow fever experiments.

Jernegan, Warren (1872–1919). Private Jernegan was the only volunteer who participated in all three phases of the team's experiments. He participated in the infected clothing and bedding experiment, the mosquito experiment (he did not get sick), and the blood injection experiments. He received the Congressional Gold Medal. He is #14 in the photo on page 66.

Kissinger, John (1877–1946). Private Kissinger, a member of the hospital corps, was in charge of the operating room at Camp Columbia when he became fascinated by the team's experiments and agreed to be bitten by infected mosquitoes. Although he initially refused to accept payment for participating in the experiments, he later changed his mind and received money for his services. He also, subsequently, received the Congressional Gold Medal. Unfortunately, Kissinger never entirely recovered from his bout of yellow fever. After spinal problems destroyed his ability to walk, Kissinger's wife supported her husband by doing laundry. Pensions from the government and from private donors eventually provided some financial relief, but, in his later years, Kissinger developed mental illness. Before dying, the former army private described his experiences in Cuba in an essay that is now part of the Hench yellow fever collection at the University of Virginia and can be read on their website. Kissinger is #10 in the photo on page 66 (see pp. 63–73).

Moran, John (1876-1950). John Moran was one of only two civilians who participated in the experiments as volunteers. Moran was born in Ireland and came to the United States as a boy. He worked in a grocery store and as an assistant to a woman doctor before enlisting in the U.S. Army Hospital Corps. After completing his army service in Cuba, he remained at Camp Columbia as a "clerk-typist-secretary." Moran never did become a doctor. After the Reed experiments ended, Moran became a sanitary inspector and helped stamp out mosquitoes during the building of the Panama Canal. He later became a businessman and served as a U.S. Army captain during World War I. Moran received the Congressional Gold Medal and also wrote several descriptions of his experiences with the team entitled "Walter Reed's Human Guinea Pigs (By One of Them)," "My Date with Walter Reed and Yellow Jack," and "Memoirs of a Human Guinea Pig"—all of which are available online through the Hench yellow fever collection at the University of Virginia (see pp. 63–75).

Olsen, William (1874–1932). Private Olsen, a member of the hospital corps, received the Congressional Gold Medal after being injected with blood from a yellow fever patient. He is #17 in the photo on page 66.

Pinto, Alva Sherman. Although he did not win a medal and his name is not usually listed, researchers know that Dr. Pinto volunteered to be bitten in some of Lazear's early experiments. His first name is sometimes listed as Albert or Alvin. He is #2 in the photo on page 66.

Sonntag, Charles (1872–1937). Sonntag, a member of the hospital corps, participated in the mosquito experiments and received the Congressional Gold Medal. He is #41 in the photo on page 66.

Weatherwalks, Edward (1874–1916). A member of the army hospital corps, Weatherwalks participated in the infected clothing and bedding experiments. After his return from Cuba, he married and had a son. Unfortunately, he died at age forty-two without knowing that he had received the Congressional Gold Medal for his services.

West, Clyde (1877–1943). Private West participated in the mosquito experiments and was awarded the Congressional Gold Medal. He is #40 in the photo on page 66.

THE SPANISH IMMIGRANT VOLUNTEERS

Benigno, Antonio. Señor Benigno was described as a cheerful man who loved eating sweet potatoes so much that Reed teasingly called him "Boniato," which means "sweet potato" in Spanish. Benigno was the first of the Spanish volunteers to get yellow fever from the bite of an infected mosquito.

Fernandez, Nicanor. Señor Fernandez took part in both the mosquito and blood injection experiments and developed yellow fever.

Martinez, José. Although he did not become sick the first time he was bitten by infected mosquitoes, Señor Martinez came down with the disease after being bitten again in a later experiment.

Presedo, Becente. Señor Presedo took part in both the mosquito and blood injection experiments and developed yellow fever.

THE REED TEAM VOLUNTEERS

Carroll, James (1854–1907). Born in England, Carroll worked as a lumberjack and soldier before studying medicine. He contracted yellow fever after a mosquito bite and his case helped explain the cause of yellow fever (see pp. 30, 34–46).

Lazear, Jesse (1866–1900). Lazear was the first member of the Reed team to do intensive mosquito research. Although he died of yellow fever during experiments, his work and illness helped answer vital questions about the disease (see pp. 26–50).

GLOSSARY OF SCIENTIFIC TERMS

AUTOPSY: the process of cutting open and examining a corpse to find out the cause of death.

BACTERIA: tiny living one-celled organisms that can be seen individually only under a microscope. Some useful types of bacteria help living creatures digest food and allow humans to make cheese and vinegar. Other harmful bacteria may cause ear infections, tonsillitis, and deadly diseases like pneumonia and tuberculosis. When people become sick with illnesses caused by bacteria, they are often treated with powerful bacteria-killing drugs called antibiotics.

BACTERIOLOGY: the study of bacteria.

CELL: a small unit of living matter that can breathe, reproduce, take in food, and eliminate waste products. A human body is composed of about a million specialized types of cells. A tiny animal called an amoeba is made up of only one. Although there are a few exceptions, most cells are so small, they can be seen only under a microscope.

CULTURE: microorganisms (such as bacteria) or body cells that have been grown in laboratory plates or tubes containing a food such as bouillon or gelatin.

HYPOTHESIS: a theory.

IMMUNE: unable to get a disease.

INCUBATOR: an ovenlike device. It is used in laboratories to keep cultures warm so that the microorganisms or body cells will grow.

LARVA: a young, immature insect that does not look like or have the same lifestyle as an adult. A mosquito larva, for example, lives in water, looks like a worm, and eats tiny plants and animals. The word *larva* refers to one young insect. Many young insects at this stage of growth are called *larvae*.

PROBOSCIS (PRONOUNCED *PRO-BOS-KISS*): an organ that looks like a nose. Although it looks like a type of nose, an insect's proboscis is used for eating, not breathing. A mosquito's proboscis, for example, contains knifelike parts that allow the bug to stab through skin and tubes that allow the insect to suck in the blood it feeds on.

SCALPEL: a special type of knife used by surgeons.

VACCINE: a substance made from killed or weakened germs that prevents a living creature from getting a particular type of sickness by forcing its body to produce disease-fighting substances. Vaccines are used to prevent people from getting illnesses such as flu, smallpox, chicken pox, yellow fever, and polio.

VIRUS: a very tiny, very simple type of germ that is so much smaller than bacteria that it usually cannot be seen under an ordinary microscope. Viruses cause colds and many other diseases such as flu, polio, yellow fever, chicken pox, smallpox, and AIDS.

CHAPTER NOTES

A Note on Sources: The story of the conquest of yellow fever has been told many times for adults, notably in several biographies of Walter Reed and in two excellent recently published books: Molly Caldwell Crosby's *The American Plague,* and *Yellow Jack* by John R. Pierce and Jim Writer. It is also the subject of *Yellow Jack,* a highly fictionalized, critically acclaimed Broadway play written by Sidney Howard in collaboration with Paul de Kruif. To me, however, the story comes through most intensely in the letters and memoirs of the people who were actually involved. I am, therefore, extremely grateful to the UCLA Biomedical Library for providing access to various published primary materials, to the New York Academy of Medicine for allowing me to view the only surviving experimental log book kept by Reed's team, and especially to the University of Virginia, which has made it possible to view the letters, documents, articles, and photographs in the magnificent Philip S. Hench Walter Reed Yellow Fever Collection online.

1. Meeting the Monster

The young man didn't feel well: This description of a severe case of yellow fever comes from multiple sources, including Downs, pp. 451–53; Kissinger, p. 3; Altman, pp. 131–32; Oldstone, p. 49; Pierce and Writer, pp. 1 and 154; Crosby, pp. 157–59, 162–65. One of the best descriptions of yellow fever, written by Dr. William Currie during the 1793 epidemic in Philadelphia, can be read in Dickerson, p. 16.

"Yellow fever [is] . . . an enemy": Pierce and Writer, p. 73, quoting Surgeon General John Woodworth's Report to Congress, Jan. 29, 1879.

By the 1890s doctors had found: Doctors knew about the existence of bacteria in the early 1890s; viruses were not discovered until later.

how to kill . . . "germs": The techniques for killing germs listed in the text are the ones known in the 1890s. Antibiotic drugs were not developed until the 1920s.

battleship Maine *blew up:* Although Spanish agents were blamed for causing the disaster at the time, many scholars now believe that the explosion was caused by an accidental spark that blew up the ship's ammunition supplies.

Their mission was to . . . find the cause of yellow fever: Although the actual order spoke vaguely about "pursuing scientific investigation with reference to the infectious diseases" in Cuba, the surgeon general of the army, George Sternberg (who was actually in charge of the mission), sent a separate letter to Walter Reed (the chief researcher) ordering him to pay "special attention to questions relating to the etiology [cause] and prevention of yellow fever." When the team arrived in Cuba, it was clear that yellow fever was the sole focus of their work. For more information, see Pierce and Writer, p. 121, and Crosby, p. 133.

2. "Feeding the Fishes"

"feeding the fishes": Letter written by Walter Reed to his wife on June 4, 1900, quoted in Blossom Reed, p. 2.

"alleviate human suffering": Letter written by Walter Reed to his wife on Dec. 31, 1900, quoted in Blossom Reed, pp. 22–23.

The experiments were unsuccessful: Reed in "The Propagation of Yellow Fever" notes that in one hundred experiments between 1881 and 1895 Finlay produced three cases of "mild albuminuric fever" (a name that indicates that these patients might have developed mild cases of yellow fever). Pierce and Writer, p. 82, say Finlay believed that he produced twelve cases of yellow fever by using infected mosquitoes. These results, however, were not accepted by the scientific community for two reasons: first, because the cases were so mild that it was not clear that the disease was actually yellow fever, and second, because Finlay's subjects were not quarantined and the experiments were done in areas where yellow fever was so prevalent that it was not clear whether Finlay's patients had gotten yellow fever from mosquitoes or another source.

"touched": Finlay, p. 94.

"crazy": Pierce and Writer, p. 81.

"useless": Letter written by Henry Hurd to Caroline Latimer on Feb. 11, 1905.

"two or three tons": Letter written by Walter Reed to his wife on June 24, 1900, quoted in Blossom Reed, p. 2.

3. Plans

Lazear would help examine the bacteria: Hench, p. 8, says that in addition to this Lazear was supposed to work on mosquito research. I have not mentioned this in the text because Hench's statement seems to be contradicted by Lazear's July 15, 1900, letter to his wife in which he expresses frustration over the team's preoccupation with *Bacillus icteroides* and says, "I . . . want to do work which may lead to the discovery of the real organism."

4. Going Nowhere

"precious wife": Letter written by Walter Reed to his wife, July 2, 1900.

"a large Cork helmet": Letter from Walter Reed to his wife, July 7, 1900.

"I have said nothing about yellow fever": Letter from Walter Reed to his wife, July 8, 1900.

"dull," . . . *"germs for their own sake":* Letter from Jesse Lazear to his wife, July 15, 1900.

team didn't seem to be taking those ideas very seriously: Reed may actually have been more interested in other avenues of research than Lazear realized. His interest, however, may have been discouraged by his boss, the surgeon general of the army, George Sternberg, who was particularly anxious to solve the problem of *Bacillus icteroides.* In a letter to Caroline Latimer (Feb. 11, 1906) Henry Hurd notes, for example, that when Reed discussed the possibility of mosquito research with Sternberg prior to going to Cuba, Sternberg called the mosquito work a "useless investigation."

"I . . . want to do work": Letter from Jesse Lazear to his wife, July 15, 1900.

5. The First Clue?

"leak": Anon., "Viral hemorrhagic fevers."

6. Bugs

Dr. Jesse Lazear had been thinking about bugs: For information on Lazear's early interest in mosquitoes, see Hench, p. 7; Crosby, p. 146; and Pierce and Writer, p. 142.

Now all four doctors were willing to admit: The importance of the Pinar del Rio incident as a first clue is clear from Reed's "The Propagation of Yellow Fever." In that article he points out that Pinar del Rio seemed to show that infected clothing and bedding did not play a role, but that the researchers suspected that some insect had flown into the guardhouse. Although there are no diaries that tell us exactly what the researchers thought and when they thought it, it is clear from other records that the thrust of the investigation changed after the Pinar del Rio incident. This incident may also have given Reed the excuse he needed to counter Sternberg's negative ideas about insect research and begin investigating the mosquito hypothesis.

possibly in late July: I have based my description of the visit to Dr. Finlay on the account in Agramonte's "Inside Story of a Great Medical Discovery" and information about Finlay's theory. It is, however, hard to tell from available sources when this important visit took place or, indeed, who was present. Researchers at the Hench Collection at the University of Virginia (see their brief biography of Jesse Lazear on their website) have suggested that Lazear visited Finlay in June and then started to grow mosquitoes from eggs that the Cuban scientist provided. Hench doesn't give a date, but he says that the visit was made by Lazear alone or possibly by Lazear and Reed. Agramonte says the team decided to concentrate on mosquito research in August and implies that the team met with Dr. Finlay as a group. Carroll, in a letter to Robert M. O'Reilly (Aug. 29, 1906) says the visit took place prior to Reed's August 2 departure for the United States. This could possibly indicate a date in July, because that would have given the team time to raise mosquitoes for the August experiments. It is, however, certainly possible that more than one meeting took place or that various members of the team met separately with Finlay at different times. Unfortunately, unless new pieces of documentation turn up, there is no way to resolve this dispute.

"cigar-shaped": Bean, p. 127.

raise . . . mosquitoes that had never been exposed to any illness: Today scientists know that female mosquitoes can pass the yellow fever germ to offspring through their eggs, but the Reed team didn't have this information.

animals didn't get yellow fever: Scientists now know that certain types of monkeys and white mice can get yellow fever, but in Reed's time people thought that the disease affected only humans.

Agramonte was not present: No one knows why Dr. Agramonte was not at this meeting. It is possible that he was consulted earlier, that he was unavailable because he was at his lab in Havana, or that the members of the team didn't bother to discuss this issue with Agramonte because his possible immunity to yellow fever meant that he would not be a good candidate for such experiments.

all three doctors were prepared to face it: In his book *Who Goes First,* Lawrence Altman suggests that Reed left for the United States the next morning because he was scared of participating in these dangerous experiments. I would note, however (and this opinion is also expressed by Pierce and Writer, p.145), that Reed's letters show that he had been planning to go home for some time before this meeting. Crosby, p. 147, also points out that because of the unreliable shipping schedules, it would have been impossible for Reed to run away suddenly. Besides, as has been mentioned in the text, Reed had already indicated his willingness to risk his life simply by coming to Cuba and carrying out experiments. Given this information, there seems to be no reason to think that Reed acted like a coward.

"a soldier's chances": Letter from James Carroll to the Editor, June 26, 1903.

7. " I Have No Such Thing"

another healthy volunteer: In addition to members of the team, another doctor, Dr. Alva Sherman Pinto (whose name is sometimes listed as Albert or Alvin), also volunteered to be bitten in these experiments. See Crosby, p. 154.

All his experiments had failed: See Pierce and Writer, p. 149, who say that at this point Lazear was about ready to give up.

"harmless": This quotation and the description of the encounter come from Agramonte's "The Inside Story," chap. 2, p. 3.

"Yellow fever" . . . "Don't be a . . . fool": The exchange between Carroll and Pinto is reported by Bean, p. 130, whose exhaustive research included interviews with descendants of many of the participants. I have also used Crosby's account of the incident.

8. Delirious?

Early in the morning: My description of this incident is derived from Agramonte, "The Inside Story," chap. 2, pp. 3–4.

fewer white cells . . . organisms that caused the illness: The information on white blood cells comes from Downs, p. 452. I am also grateful to Dr. Martha Sonnenberg (e-mail communication Apr. 19, 2007) for helping me to understand how difficult it might have been for James Carroll to diagnose malaria when he peered through the microscope that morning.

"caught cold": Agramonte, "The Inside Story," chap. 2, p. 4.

In a state bordering on panic: Agramonte in "The Inside Story," chap. 2, p. 4, says he and Lazear were almost "panic-stricken."

"You still fooling with mosquitoes": The dialogue and the description of the incident come from Agramonte's "The Inside Story," chap. 1, p. 2.

Some people, however, have disputed the truth of Agramonte's account, which was written after Carroll and Lazear had died. Carroll, who apparently disliked Agramonte, once said that Agramonte knew nothing about the earliest mosquito experiments. Truby in his *Memoir of Walter Reed,* p. 119, says he believes Lazear would never have allowed Dean to volunteer for the experiments without explaining the potential dangers to him. The truth, however, will never be known unless other documents come to light.

"Patient delirious": Warner, p. 1.

9. "Did the Mosquito Do It?"

"I cannot begin to describe"; "Can it be that": Both quotations from a letter written by Walter Reed to Jefferson Kean, Sept. 6, 1900.

"My Dear Carroll": Letter from Walter Reed to James Carroll, Sept. 7, 1900, quoted in Hemmeter, p. 162, and Crosby, p. 160. Crosby gives a fuller rendering.

"I rather think": Fragment of letter written by Jesse Lazear, Sept. 8, 1900.

10. "Doctor, Are You Sick?"

big lab notebook . . . smaller book: The big lab notebook can still be seen at the New York Academy of Medicine. The smaller notebook was given to Reed after Lazear died, but it disappeared after Reed's own death.

"Guinea pig No. 1": Log Book of the Yellow Fever Commission, p. 100.

Nobody will . . . ever know: It is possible that the answers to some of these questions were contained in Lazear's small lab notebook, which later disappeared. In the absence of concrete evidence, however, many people have tried to guess why Lazear might have lied about the bite. Pierce and Writer have suggested that Lazear concealed it because Reed may have ordered the young man to stop all human experiments after Carroll's illness. I have not mentioned this theory in the text because, first, there is no evidence that Reed actually did this, and, second, because in the light of Reed's later willingness to engage in human experiments, it seems unlikely that he would have issued such an order. Another theory states that Lazear might have been afraid his insurance company would have canceled benefits if they had known that he was risking his life in these experiments. I have mentioned this possibility even though Altman points out that there is no evidence that Lazear owned such a policy because the theory seems to make sense and because there is also no proof that Lazear *did not* own this type of policy. I do think it is possible that Lazear didn't want his family to know that he was risking his life, and I also wonder if Lazear's colleagues knew more about his "secret" than they ever said.

"nervous"; "flushed"; eyes were red: The dialogue and description of this incident all come from Kissinger, p. 4. Truby, *Memoir of Walter Reed,* p. 117, says that Lazear did not work late, but both Kissinger and Lazear's nurse, Lena Warner (quoted in Kelly, *Walter Reed and Yellow Fever,* p. 236), stated that Lazear was up all night writing reports. I have followed their accounts.

"I can but believe": Letter from Walter Reed to James Carroll, Sept. 24, 1900.

flash of panic: for documentation of this incident see Kelly, *Walter Reed and Yellow Fever,* p. 284, and a letter from James Carroll to Caroline Latimer dated Mar. 9, 1905.

8:45 that evening: Some writers have stated that Lazear died at 8:45 a.m. This, I believe, is due to a misreading of the entry on Lazear's temperature chart in the Hench Collection at the University of Virginia.

"Dr. Lazear died": Telegram from Jefferson Kean to Mabel Lazear, Sept. 26, 1900, in the Hench Collection at the University of Virginia.

11. Sorting It Out

"terribly depressed": Truby, *Memoir of Walter Reed,* p. 116. Truby's assessment of Reed's feelings has weight because the two men were in contact during the period immediately following Lazear's death.

first two cases didn't "prove": Letter from Walter Reed to James Carroll, Sept. 24, 1900; Reed's italics.

"My man": The quotations and the description of this interview are taken from Truby, *Memoir of Walter Reed,* p. 122. Truby knew Walter Reed and was stationed at Camp Columbia at the time of this incident.

germs had to stay in the mosquito's body: Scientists now know that after the mosquito sucks in the yellow fever germ, a series of changes takes place in the insect's cells over the course of seven to seventeen days that allow the germ to enter the mosquito's salivary glands (the glands that produce saliva). When the mosquito bites again, it pumps this germ-laden saliva into its new victim. The germ can also enter the mosquito's eggs during this period, and that allows the bug to pass on the infection to a new generation of insects.

"General Wood": The description of this incident and all quotations come from Jefferson Kean's account of the meeting with Wood, in Blossom Reed, p. 5.

two hundred and fifty thousand dollars: This calculation was done through E.H. Net Economic History Service.

"From our study": Reed et al., "The Etiology of Yellow Fever: A Preliminary Note," p. 53.

"pure speculation": Bean, p. 143, quoting the *Philadelphia Medical Journal.*

"Of all the silly": Anon., "The Mosquito Hypothesis."

12. Problems

tried to cheer him up: The description of this incident comes from Truby, *Memoir of Walter Reed,* pp. 143–44. Truby was with Reed at lunch that day and was one of the young doctors who went bug hunting.

dosed unsuspecting patients with disease germs: Experimenting on unsuspecting patients was quite common a century ago. Pierce and Writer, p. 175, note, for example, that Sanarelli didn't get permission from his experimental subjects and that three of those individuals died after being injected with *Bacillus icteroides.* It is also interesting to note that although physicians have long believed in the principles of the two-thousand-year-old Hippocratic Oath (which asks doctors to swear that they will not deliberately harm a patient), history shows that physicians have also struggled to balance this belief with the fact that it is necessary to endanger a few lives in order to discover a fact that may save thousands. Dr. Lawrence Altman in *Who Goes First,* p. 15, sums up this problem by pointing out that "a literal interpretation" of the Hippocratic Oath would put a stop to most medical research.

"deliberately injecting a poison": Altman, p. 135, quoting William Osler in "Discussion of G.M. Sternberg, 'The Bacillus Icteroides (Sanarelli) and Bacillus X (Sternberg).'" *Transactions of the Association of American Physicians 13 no. 71: (1898).*

he wanted to do something new: Walter Reed's belief that all volunteers should be fully informed of the risks before participating in scientific experiments has had an important effect on medical research. Today, thanks in part to Reed's work, the thousands of people who help U.S. doctors test new drugs and treatments are legally required to sign a form that specifically explains the possible dangers before taking part in any experiments.

13. "We Are Doing It for Medical Science"

$2,400: This calculation was done through E.H. Net Economic History Service.

"Just think, Johnny": All quotations and the account of this incident have been derived from Moran, "Memoirs of a Human Guinea Pig," pp. 7–9, and Moran, Draft fragments: "Walter Reed's Human Guinea Pigs," p. 3.

"I take my hat off"; "I salute you": "I take my hat off" comes from a letter from Henry Hurd to Caroline Latimer, Feb. 2, 1906. "I salute you" comes from Kelly, *Walter Reed and Yellow Fever,* p. 139. Both these responses, which come from secondary sources, are unlikely to be true. See Pierce and Writer, p. 177, for a discussion.

"gladly accepted": Moran, "Memoirs of a Human Guinea Pig," p. 9.

"courage . . . has never been surpassed": Reed, "The Propagation of Yellow Fever," p. 98.

14. Testing Times

"I shall regret": Letter from Walter Reed to George Sternberg, Jan. 31, 1901.

15. More Bugs

weather had somehow affected the mosquitoes: Although cold may affect the amount of time the yellow fever germ has to stay inside a mosquito before that insect can infect another individual, Pierce and Writer have pointed out that some of the early experiments may not have worked because the mosquitoes were not properly infected. Scientists now know, as the Reed team did not, that an insect must bite a yellow fever victim in the first three days of the illness in order to pick up the germ that causes the disease.

"I felt . . . as though six Ford cars": Quotation and description of the incident from Kissinger, p. 3.

"It is with a great deal"; "Rejoice with me": Letter from Walter Reed to his wife, Dec. 9, 1900.

"Merry Christmas, Moran": Moran, Draft fragments: "Walter Reed's Human Guinea Pigs," p. 6.

16. Celebration

"with many blushes": Letter from Walter Reed to his wife, Dec. 26, 1900, in Blossom Reed, p. 21.

"11:50 p.m. Dec 31": Letter from Walter Reed to his wife, Dec. 31, 1900, in Blossom Reed, pp. 22–23.

Someday, Reed hoped: By mentioning that he hoped twentieth-century scientists would find a cure for yellow fever in his Dec. 31, 1900, letter to his wife, Reed makes it clear that he looked forward for further research. Crosby, p. 182, also indicates that Reed was planning to do additional research himself.

Epilogue

"Vaccinations!": Amarilla, p. A4.

PHOTO CREDITS

Unless otherwise noted in the text, all photos have been obtained from the following sources:

Centers for Disease Control and Prevention: pp. 19, 37, 38, 59, 60, 75 (photo by James Gathany), 85.

Dennis Kunkel Microscopy, Inc.: pp. 29, 79.

Historical Collections & Services, Claude Moore Health Sciences Library, University of Virginia: frontispiece (Lazear, Finlay, and Reed), pp. 8, 9, 12–13, 15, 16, 18, 20, 27, 42–43, 44, 45, 47, 50, 52, 58, 64, 65, 66, 69, 71, 73, 74.

Library of Congress: pp. 4, 5, 14, 25, 55, 80, 82.

National Library of Medicine: frontispiece (Agramonte and Carroll), pp. 2, 21, 23, 28, 32, 33, 61, 68, 72, 83, 84.

Richard B. Jurmain: p. 78.

Superior Galleries: p. 81.

BIBLIOGRAPHY

Note: Writing this book would have been impossible without online access to the wonderful Philip S. Hench Walter Reed Yellow Fever Collection at the University of Virginia (http://yellowfever.lb.virginia.edu/reed/collection.html), which includes a rich and searchable array of documents, letters, articles, and photographs. In order to save space, the title of this source has been abbreviated as Hench Coll., University of Virginia, in the entries that follow.

Agramonte, Aristides. "A Statement Regarding the Work Carried Out by the Army Board, August 31, 1908." Hench Coll., University of Virginia.

———. "The Inside Story of a Great Medical Discovery," World Wide School Library, Seattle, Washington, 1998 (www.worldwideschool.org/library/books/tech/medicine/YellowFever/chap1.html; www.worldwideschool.org/library/books/tech/medicine/YellowFever/chap2.html).

Altman, Lawrence K. *Who Goes First: The Story of Self-Experimentation in Medicine.* Berkeley: University of California Press, 1998.

Amarilla, Pablo. "Vaccine short, Paraguay in panic over yellow fever," *Los Angeles Times,* Feb. 25, 2008, p. A4.

Andrus, John H. "I Become a Guinea Pig: An Episode from Big Moments in a Little Life—A Report." Hench Coll., University of Virginia.

Anon. "A Hero from the Ranks," *Outlook,* June 29, 1907. Hench Coll., University of Virginia.

———. Consent form for Antonio Benigno. Hench Coll., University of Virginia.

———. Log Book of the Yellow Fever Commission's work. New York Academy of Medicine, Rare Book Collection.

———. "Mosquito Carries Yellow Fever," *New York Times,* Oct. 27, 1900. Hench Coll., University of Virginia.

———. Special order #25, Aug. 22, 1900. Hench Coll., University of Virginia.

———. "Student of Yellow Fever," *Chicago Record,* 1900. Hench Coll., University of Virginia.

———. "The Mosquito Hypothesis," *Washington Post,* Nov. 2, 1900. Hench Coll., University of Virginia.

———. "The Southern Epidemic," *New York Times,* Oct. 8, 1878.

———. "Viral hemorrhagic fevers" from MayoClinic.com special to CNN.com (www.cnn.com/HEALTH/library/DS/00539.html).

Bean, William B. *Walter Reed: A Biography.* Charlottesville: University Press of Virginia, 1982.

Blum, John M., William S. McFeely, Edward S. Morgan, Arthur M. Schlesinger, Jr., Kenneth M. Stampp, and C. Vann Woodward. *The National Experience: A History of the United States,* 6th ed. San Diego: Harcourt Brace Jovanovich, 1985.

Bruce-Chwatt, L. J. "Malaria" in the *Cecil-Loeb Textbook of Medicine,* 13th ed., vol. 1, edited by Paul B. Beeson and Walsh McDermott. Philadelphia: W. B. Saunders, 1971.

Carroll, James. Correspondence. Hench Coll., University of Virginia.

———. "Yellow Fever: A Popular Lecture on Yellow Fever" in *Yellow Fever: A Compendium of Various Publications: The Results of the Work of Major Walter Reed,* Medical Corps, United States Army and the Yellow Fever Commission, 1911. Hench Coll., University of Virginia.

————. "Report to the Surgeon General on Yellow Fever" in *Yellow Fever: A Compendium of Various Publications: Results of the Work of Major Walter Reed,* Medical Corps., United States Army and the Yellow Fever Commission, 1911. Hench Coll., University of Virginia.

Crosby, Molly Caldwell. *The American Plague: The Untold Story of Yellow Fever, The Epidemic That Shaped Our History.* New York: Berkeley Books (Penguin), 2006.

De Kruif, Paul. *Microbe Hunters.* New York: Pocket Books, 1964.

Dickerson, James L. *Yellow Fever: A Deadly Disease Poised to Kill Again.* Amherst, N.Y.: Prometheus Books, 2006.

Downs, Wilbur. "Yellow Fever" in the *Cecil-Loeb Textbook of Medicine,* 13th ed., vol. 1, edited by Paul B. Beeson and Walsh McDermott. Philadelphia: W. B. Saunders, 1971.

E.H. Net Economic History Service (eh.net/hmit).

Finlay, Carlos E., Morton C. Kahn, ed. *Carlos Finlay and Yellow Fever.* New York: Institute of Tropical Medicine of the University of Havana by the Oxford University Press, 1940.

Hemmeter, John C. "Major James Carroll of the United States Army, Yellow Fever Commission, and the Discovery of the Transmission of Yellow Fever by the Bite of the Mosquito 'Stegomyia Fasciata.'" 1908. Hench Coll., University of Virginia.

Hench, Philip S. "The Conquest of Yellow Fever," manuscript for an illustrated talk, Jan. 31, 1955. Hench Coll., University of Virginia.

Howard, Sidney, and Paul de Kruif. *Yellow Jack in Three Plays About Doctors,* edited by Joseph Mersand. New York: Washington Square Press, 1961.

Hurd, Henry, M. Correspondence. Hench Coll., University of Virginia.

Kean, Jefferson R. "Major Reed as a Medical Officer," in *Yellow Fever: A Compendium of Various Publications: Results of the Work of Major Walter Reed, Medical Corps., United States Army, and the Yellow Fever Commission,* 1911. Hench Coll., University of Virginia.

————. Note by Jefferson Kean in L.O. Howard, report excerpt in *A History of Applied Entomology,* p. 1, 1930. Hench Coll., University of Virginia.

Kelly, Howard A. "The Lesson of Little Things: The Conquest of Yellow Fever." *Youth's Companion* 81, no. 2. Hench Coll., University of Virginia

————. *Walter Reed and Yellow Fever,* 2nd ed. Baltimore: Medical Standard Book Co., 1906.

King, A.F.A. "Dr. Walter Reed as a Teacher" in *Yellow Fever: A Compendium of Various Publications: Results of the Work of Major Walter Reed, Medical Corps., United States Army, and the Yellow Fever Commission,* 1911. Hench Coll., University of Virginia.

Kissinger, John R. "Experiences with the Yellow Fever Commission in Cuba 1900." Hench Coll., University of Virginia.

Lazear, Jesse. Correspondence. Hench Coll., University of Virginia.

Lazear, Mabel. Correspondence. Hench Coll., University of Virginia.

McCaw, Walter D. "Walter Reed: A Memoir" in *Yellow Fever: A Compendium of Various Publications: Results of the Work of Major Walter Reed, Medical Corps., United States Army, and the Yellow Fever Commission,* 1911. Hench Coll., University of Virginia.

Moran, John J. Draft fragments: "Walter Reed's Human Guinea Pigs (By One of Them)." Hench Coll., University of Virginia.

———. "My Date with Walter Reed and Yellow Jack." Hench Coll., University of Virginia.

———. "Memoirs of a Human Guinea Pig." Hench Coll., University of Virginia.

Oldstone, Michael. *Viruses, Plagues and History.* New York: Oxford University Press, 1998.

Peabody, James. Correspondence. Hench Coll., University of Virginia.

Pierce, John, and Jim Writer. *Yellow Jack: How Yellow Fever Ravaged America and Walter Reed Discovered Its Deadly Secrets.* Hoboken, N.J.: John Wiley & Sons, 2005.

Powell, J. H. *Bring Out Your Dead: The Great Plague of Yellow Fever in Philadelphia in 1793.* Philadelphia: University of Pennsylvania Press, 1949.

Reed, Blossom [Emilie M.]. "Biographical Sketch: Life and Letters of Dr. Walter Reed." Hench Coll., University of Virginia.

Reed, Walter. Correspondence. Hench Coll., University of Virginia.

———. "The Propagation of Yellow Fever— Observations Based on Recent Researches" in *Yellow Fever: A Compendium of Various Publications: Results of the Work of Major Walter Reed, Medical Corps., United States Army, and the Yellow Fever Commission,* 1911. Hench Coll., University of Virginia.

Reed, Walter, James Carroll, Aristides Agramonte, and Jesse Lazear. "The Etiology of Yellow Fever: A Preliminary Note." Paper presented at a meeting of the American Public Health Association in Indianapolis, Oct. 23, 1900. Hench Coll., University of Virginia.

Reed, Walter, James Carroll, and Aristides Agramonte. "The Etiology of Yellow Fever—An Additional Note" in *Yellow Fever: A Compendium of Various Publications: Results of the Work of Major Walter Reed, Medical Corps., United States Army, and the Yellow Fever Commission,* 1911. Hench Coll., University of Virginia.

Sternberg, George M. *A Text-Book of Bacteriology.* New York: William Wood, 1896.

Tripp, David E. "Congressional Gold Medal for the Conquest of Yellow Fever Awarded to Edward Weatherwalks." Draft of article later published in the Superior Galleries, Beverly Hills catalogue, for the sale of the above mentioned medal, Sept. 10–12, 2006.

Truby, Albert E. Article extracts. Hench Coll., University of Virginia.

———. *Memoir of Walter Reed: The Yellow Fever Episode.* New York: Paul B. Hoeber, 1943.

Warner, Lena. "The Experiment with Yellow Fever," June 1902. Hench Coll., University of Virginia.

Wills, Christopher. *Yellow Fever Black Goddess: The Coevolution of People and Plagues.* New York: Basic Books, 1996.

Further Reading

Young readers who would like to know what a yellow fever epidemic was like should read these two books:

Anderson, Laurie Halse. *Fever, 1793.* New York: Aladdin, 2002. (fiction)

Murphy, Jim. *An American Plague: The True and Terrifying Story of the Yellow Fever Epidemic of 1793.* New York: Clarion, 2003. (nonfiction)

INDEX

Illustration page references appear in *italics*. Glossary terms appear in **boldface**.